Reaching the
Interactive
Customer

Integrated Services for
the Digital World

MAI-LAN TOMSEN

RON FAITH

CAMBRIDGE
UNIVERSITY PRESS

PUBLISHED BY THE PRESS SYNDICATE OF THE UNIVERSITY OF CAMBRIDGE
The Pitt Building, Trumpington Street, Cambridge, United Kingdom

CAMBRIDGE UNIVERSITY PRESS
The Edinburgh Building, Cambridge CB2 2RU, UK
40 West 20th Street, New York, NY 10011-4211, USA
477 Williamstown Road, Port Melbourne, VIC 3207, Australia
Ruiz de Alarcón 13, 28014 Madrid, Spain
Dock House, The Waterfront, Cape Town 8001, South Africa

http://www.cambridge.org

First published 2003

Printed in the United States of America

Typeface Garamond 3 12/14.5 pt.   *System* LaTeX 2_ε [TB]

A catalog record for this book is available from the British Library.

Library of Congress Cataloging in Publication Data available

ISBN 0 521 81670 X paperback

To our spouses, Brandi and Mark, and our youngest interactive customers, Nicholas, Ian, Derek, and Hailey.

Contents

Acknowledgements

This book is written at an exciting time in the evolution of consumer technologies. As the Internet phenomenon created often unrealistic expectations, Web-based applications also stand as one of the most constructively disruptive technologies in the history of the world. While we do not yet know the full impact of the Internet on society, it clearly continues the evolution of digital, networked technologies into our daily lives.

Having lived in the high-tech industry for all of our professional lives, we are indebted to a great number of people who have influenced our views while at both Apple and Microsoft. We would like to thank management at Microsoft and Qpass for their flexibility in enabling us to take on this project. Other people who influenced some of the thinking that went into this book include Mark McNeely, for his creative thoughts around consumer's continued adoption of technology; Bert Kolde, for leading by example in nimble and creative thinking; Carey Heckman, for his insights into technology, the law, and public policy; and Kendra VanderMeulen, for her extensive knowledge of the past, present, and future of the wireless industry. Finally, we would like to thank each other for being supportive during a hectic time in both of our lives (with new babies and late nights). We are excited that we are on this journey together, experiencing the evolution of integrated services from novelty to necessity in our daily lives.

About the Authors

Mai-lan Tomsen is the author of *Killer Content: Strategies for Web Content and Ecommerce* (Addison Wesley Longman, 2000), a popular guide for business and technical managers struggling to implement revenue-generating content on Web sites. Currently working at Microsoft, she recently led the ecommerce team at digeo, a leading digital services provider to cable network operators.

Ron Faith has a decade of experience in interactive technologies and is the Vice President of Business Development for Qpass, creators of mobile and broadband activity management systems. As a Program Manager of Internet Products at Apple Computer, he specified and launched Apple's first consumer Internet product, the Apple Internet Connection Kit, and oversaw product integration relationships with Netscape, Adobe, and Real Networks.

Permeation of the Information Age

D igital devices, complex networks, and interactive applications and services permeate our daily routines. The adoption of digital, integrated services in peoples' lives stems from a causal chain involving customers of new technologies, device designers, and application product planners. Consumer expectations, set by the growing capabilities of interactive devices, fuel innovation from application and service product planners. Product planners then push the device designers to accommodate their increasingly sophisticated features (see Figure 1-1). The key to continual improvement without costly design mistakes lies in understanding how the consumers' expectations evolve with usage.

For example, cell phones with Internet access influence the consumers' expectations about repurposing the phone for other uses. However, browsing the Internet on a cell phone is a frustrating experience due to the limited screen display. Application and service designers step in to meet consumers' expectations of Internet access with alternatives to Web browsing. Internet-based applications deliver discrete amounts of information suited to the cell phone's screen display, such as personalized weather and stock quotes. Internet-based instant messaging and chat allow consumers the ability to use the phone's small screen for shorthand text messages. The adoption of these types of services and applications provides incentive for device designers to develop new features to accommodate the different usage.

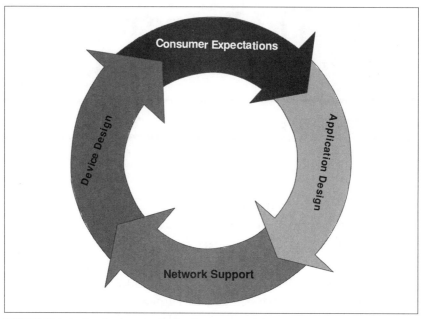

FIGURE 1-1. Evolutionary Cycle for Interactive Devices

The evolutionary cycle for interactive devices moves as fast as the device manufacturers and application providers release new variations of the product. As consumers become familiar with new interactive features, the consumer develops new expectations about the device itself and services and networks that support the service. The need to fulfill these shifting expectations results in an acceleration of the development cycle for device manufacturers and service providers. An accelerated speed of development can result in poor, costly design decisions. Balancing speed against market demands and accurate design requires an in-depth understanding of how interactive consumer expectations drive the evolution of technology. Starting with the consumer and the expectations of the consumer helps device designers and application and service planners to prioritize features and deliver successful products.

Understanding consumer expectations begins with understanding how consumers use (and don't use) technologies. Digital devices

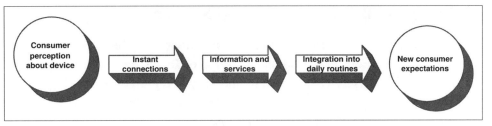

FIGURE 1-2. Changing Consumer Expectations Through Usage

and communication networks provide instant connections to other people, applications, and services. Consumers use these services to gain access to a world of limitless repositories of digitized information and media. The dual forces of instant connection and access to limitless information propel deeper adoption of integrated services in consumers' daily routines (see Figure 1-2).

Based on their dependency on the device, consumers who incorporate integrated services into daily routines expect greater capabilities from their devices. This book describes how device, application, and service providers can take advantage of and drive these new consumer expectations. By breaking down consumer expectations for different types of interactive experiences (like audio and visual), technology providers gain a better understanding of the customer for devices and services.

First, let's lay the foundation for understanding the interactive consumer by discussing the relationship between devices, services, and applications in an integrated service. This chapter describes the following:

▣ The definition of an "integrated service"

▣ How instant access and limitless information results in the adoption of new integrated services

▣ How digital networks and devices enable new forms of communication

Components of an Integrated Service

The options available to consumers today cannot easily be classified in traditional notions of a product or a service. Today, most interactive products have a service component and most integrated services have a product component. An integrated service combines products and services into a single package for the user.

Integrated services consist of the following three tiers:

- Devices

- Networks

- Applications and services

Each of the three tiers has different technologies and business models. Each tier provides value to the consumer in a way that would be difficult to achieve independently. For example, a cell phone without access to an Internet network has a very different consumer value proposition than a cell phone with Internet network access and a game application. The combination of the three tiers, as depicted in Figure 1-3, creates the most compelling package, which in turn raises consumer expectations for each tier in the integrated service.

Devices are the first and most tangible tier to the consumer. Devices take many forms and come with a wide range of capabilities. A device can be stationary in a given location (e.g., personal computers, cable television set-top boxes, and gaming consoles) or a device can also travel with the consumer [e.g., a cell phone or a personal digital assistant (PDA)].

Most interactive devices share the three following common characteristics:

1. The device has a user interface through which the consumer interacts with the device.

2. The device can connect to data communications networks.

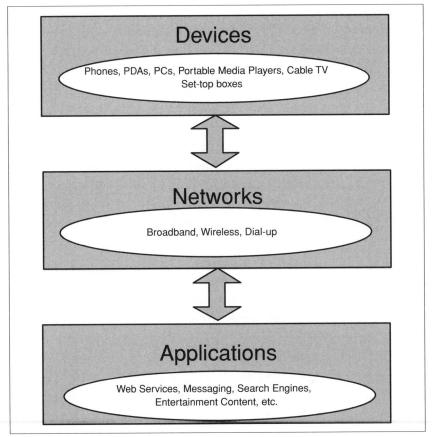

FIGURE 1-3. Integrated Service Tiers

3. The device has computing capabilities such as a microprocessor and memory.

These characteristics support the enhanced features that change consumer expectations about the device.

Devices play a crucial role in an integrated service by serving as the tangible touch point for the consumer. The consumer sees the device as the point of access to a digital world. Without the device, the other tiers in integrated services are hard pressed to deliver value to the consumer. At the same time, devices need the other tiers to offer consumers new, exciting features that depend on access to communication, computing, and data resources. Data communication networks comprise the second tier in the integrated service. Devices need to be connected to a network in order to communicate with other devices or with application and data servers. Devices exchange data in digital formats through data communication networks. (Chapter 3 talks in more detail about the evolution from analog to digital networks.) Traditional telecommunication providers, wireless carriers, and cable television service operators have built out large, consumer-oriented data networks to support the next generation of integrated services.

Application and service providers form the third and final tier of the integrated service. This tier offers a wide diversity of options for the consumer to use the device and networks. Applications and services also act as a tool for service providers such as cable companies to help foster lasting relationships with consumers. Services in the third tier span the spectrum of entertainment, governmental, informational, and financial services. Examples include MSN Hotmail for email, eBay for auctions, and Amazon.com for retail. Application and service providers host their own applications and provide features to end users in exchange for subscription fees and pay-per-use fees or by having the value subsidized through sponsorship.

Successful integrated services take advantage of each of these tiers to provide an integrated product to the consumer.

Targeting the Interactive Consumer

The interactive consumer is a constantly moving target. Designers of interactive products must not only understand what the consumer has always expected from a product but also predict how those expectations will evolve. Using the device creates a whole new set of consumer expectations that need to be met by the next generation of devices, networks, and services. For the companies providing these new devices, networks, and service, understanding the evolutionary trends for the interactive consumer can mitigate the risks inherent in bring expensive new devices and infrastructures to market.

Interactive consumers possess common traits and characteristics. As a group, interactive consumers include almost all members of society. By 2002, 58 percent of all Americans ages twelve and older owned a mobile phone. One of every three adults ages eighteen and older plays computer games. The adoption rate for integrated services in the home points to how quickly integrated services become part of household life. It also demonstrates the interdependence of the three tiers in an integrated service. Consider the relationship between personal computers, the Internet, and Internet-based applications. One prominent consumer research firm found that by the end of 2001, 67.4 million U.S. households owned a personal computer (PC). Personal computer ownership in turn fostered the consumers' desire to be connected to a network (the Internet). About 94 percent of households with PCs also had Internet access.[1] This Internet access in turn spawned development of online applications and services. A recent Forrester Research survey found that 94 percent of the people surveyed used email at least once a week with almost equal usage across demographics and age groups.[2] Fifty-four percent entered Internet-based sweepstakes and competitions. Thirty-one percent of PC owners used their computers for playing games daily. As integrated services become part of daily routines, consumers begin to expect to expect more from the device—the PC evolves in the household from a word processor to an interactive gateway to people

1. Forrester Research, Inc., Consumer Survey, "Forrester's Consumer Technographics 2002 North America Benchmark Study," Boston: Forrester Research, Inc., 2002.
2. Forrester Research, Inc., Consumer Survey, "Devices & Access, 2002 Online Survey," Boston: Forrester Research, Inc., 2002.

and products. The changing expectations in turn drive the PC manufacturers to build faster devices with more audio and video capabilities.

Keeping up with evolving consumer expectations requires an understanding of what the consumer wants to get out of the ownership of the device. Consumers who own interactive devices use the technology to *enhance* the consumer's lifestyle. The consumer buys the device to facilitate personal preferences. Device selection becomes a reflection of the buyer's personal style. As a result, many designers create phones and other devices that target demographics and age groups. Likewise, application and service providers give consumers more options for personalization and customization in the services accessed via the devices. Consumers want control over the incorporation of interactive technologies in their lives.

It's important for device and application product planners to understand that the average interactive consumer is not drawn to an integrated service purely for the technology. Only "early adopters" of new devices (a small demographic in the total potential market) are drawn by the lure of the technology. The average consumer adopts an integrated service because the technology enables an end goal— perhaps to be more productive, reinforce a sense of identity, or stay connected to important people. Integrating an integrated service into a consumer's lifestyle often translates into the consumer's growing dependence on "instant connections"—the ability to always access information and services via a device.

Instant Connections

High-speed networks form the backbone of instant access to information. The Internet exemplifies how a network enables the dissemination of information to consumers. Millions of documents live on the World Wide Web, providing a combination of fact and fiction for consumers to access via interactive devices like the PC and

Web-enabled cell phones. On-demand information can entertain, inform, and educate the consumer's daily life. Access to information from interactive devices changes how providers disseminate information and consumers use it.

For example, many potential car buyers turn to online information sites like www.carpoint.com to compare, contrast, and learn about all aspects of automobiles and financing. Most consumers still prefer to buy a car from a car dealership rather than through an online service, due to the size of the transaction and the desire to test drive. In 2001 only 300,000 buyers purchased their vehicles from online dealerships, less than 0.5 percent of the total households online.[3] Car research sites are popular destination sites for car enthusiasts and potential purchasers. Car research sites provide users with extensive information on new car models, model comparison tools, trade-in values for old cars, and pricing tools that help buyers see the full cost of a vehicle with options. As a result, more informed consumers come to car dealerships armed with detailed information about the purchase. Therefore, taking a test drive can mark the end rather than the beginning of the buying process. The overall transaction time can be significantly reduced (and simplified) if the buyer comes to the car dealership with more information for the purchase decisions. The easy availability of information makes it easy for consumers to integrate on-demand information into daily routines as well as facilitate large purchases like an automobile. For example, interactive devices like Web-enabled PDAs give consumers the ability to access information from any location. Consumers can check stock quotes and execute a stock trade while waiting in line at the airport. This level of access facilitates the integration of the integrated service to the consumer's lifestyle. Online auctions demonstrate how an integrated

3. Kelley, Christopher M. "Retail & Media April 2002 Data Overview: Covers Email Marketing, eCommerce Growth, And Print Media Cannibalization," Boston: Forrester Research, Inc., April 2002.

service achieves success by giving control to the consumer. In the past when people participated in a physical auction, they traveled to attend the auction and place their bids. Now, using interactive devices like a mobile phone or a personal computer, people can participate in online auctions from wherever there is network access. This ease of access makes online auctions simple to integrate into a person's schedule. In fact, one consumer survey found that over one quarter of all online consumers had bid in an online auction.[4] The ability to access information from any location at any time makes the consumer, rather than the physical location of the information, the center of the experience.

The "Digital Lifestyle"

Consumers grow to depend on obtaining information and services at their own convenience. The "digital lifestyle," while a popular phrase, is a misnomer. People simply have lifestyles and choose to use technology to augment their lifestyles. While early adopters may adopt technology for technology's sake, the mainstream does not. Average people adopt interactive technology into their lives when it increases their productivity, reinforces a sense of identity, or maintains connections with others. Mainstream consumers value what *can be done* with the technology rather than the technology itself.

Consumers' lives are becoming increasingly dependent on digital devices, networks, and services. The combined forces of instant connections and access to limitless information enable people to be more productive and intensify the pursuit of personal interests. Let's take a look at how integrated services increase a consumer's expectations around hobbies, education, and communication.

---

4. Kelley, Christopher M. "Retail & Media September 2001 Data Overview: Covers Retail Channels, Online Advertising, Online Auctions, And Delivery," Boston: Forrester Research, Inc., April 2002.

Hobby Central

We all possess a concept of our own identity. As people change jobs and geographic locations more frequently, a person's identity and associations become increasingly defined by the affinity to particular interests rather than to a location. The Internet provides a common communication medium for communities to share interests. The Internet also changes a consumer's expectations around participating in that interest and community. Before the advent of interactive devices and networks, genealogists (people who study ancestry and family heritage) spent a considerable amount of time investigating courthouse records and public institution files. Integrated services, like those offered by Ancestory.com, facilitate locating and displaying information about family histories.

Ancestory.com is a genealogy Web service that is part of the MyFamily.com group of services. Web services such as Ancestory.com provide novice to advanced researchers in genealogy with access to research repositories. Ancestory.com has a repository of over a billion names from over 3,000 databases such as the Social Security Death Index and the U.S. Census Bureau. Sites like Ancestory.com make it possible for hobbyists to enhance their participation in the hobby. In the case of Ancestory.com, there are over 500,000 paid subscribers to the genealogy service.

The combination of access and information helps the hobbyist explore his or her interests in a more effective manner. As a result, the hobbyist comes to expect more from the integrated service (in our example, the genealogy research site) itself. Instead of simply providing access to information to form a family history, interactive consumers demand more features, such as community chat rooms, to discuss research techniques and online templates to display family trees. The evolution of consumer expectations drives service providers such as Ancestory.com to add additional features that support the consumer's dependency on the site.

Learning Center

An increasing number of jobs require continuous learning of new skills in a given area. The traditional education system focused on the full-time student at a centralized location. That framework did not easily accommodate the professional looking for continuing education. Learning institutions use the combination of connectivity and information to provide a new educational integrated service: distance learning. Networked, integrated services form the backbone of distance learning. Through email, Web applications, and download sites, the teacher and students are able to discuss assignments and address questions. Online information resources provide a virtual library for students researching a paper. Online bookstores make it possible for the student to quickly and easily order the books for his or her next term's classes. Students submit assignments to the teacher or professor via email or use the Internet to take an online test.

The student participates in the distance learning according to his or her own schedule, in contrast to appearing in a classroom according to a course schedule. Professionals can participate at times that do not conflict with their professional obligations. As an integrated service, distance learning allows the consumer to choose how to integrate the integrated service with his or her own lifestyle.

The University of Phoenix provides one example of a distance learning integrated service. The University of Phoenix is a fully accredited university with extension campuses around the United States, Canada, and Puerto Rico. What makes the University of Phoenix unique is their intense focus on continuing education for professionals. The University of Phoenix began providing its Internet-based degree programs in 1989. Professionals can put in ten to twenty hours of coursework per week toward a degree, without needing to co-reside with the university.

The classes themselves are available over the Internet. Students retrieve lectures, questions, and assignments from their instructor to review. Students also have access to a range of online research libraries and services. Adoption of this continuing education approach has been dramatic. Since 1978, the University of Phoenix has grown to be the largest private university in the United States. Students choose from purely online integrated services or blend their online studies with on-site classes given at over 116 distributed campuses. The integrated service combines applications like email, Web-based applications with a dependency on devices such as the personal computer, and data communication networks. The result fosters new expectations about a consumer-focused education, with the consumer determining the schedule and participation format for classes.

Family Connections

Prior to the Internet, people stayed in touch with family and friends through written letters, through the spoken word over the phone, and in face-to-face meetings. Digital communication networks give consumers new ways to communicate. The adoption of the cell phone shifts communications from a location-to-location transmission to a person-to-person transmission. A person's phone number becomes tied to a person's account rather than to the person's location.

New digital networks now enable the mobile phone to support many modes of communication from one device. Data-capable mobile phones and networks transport voice and data communications in synchronous and asynchronous modes. Synchronous communication involves people communicating at the same time, such as having a conversation on the phone. Asynchronous communications occurs when people communicate with one another at different points in time, such as through email or a written letter. Digital networks support both synchronous and asynchronous forms of communication and bridge multiple forms of communication. For example, modern data-capable mobile phones support not only voice-based synchronous communications but also text-based asynchronous communications through the use of the simple mail service (SMS) protocol. For example, billions of short text messages are sent between mobile phones in Europe and Asia.

On personal computers and many data-capable communication devices, communication applications provide capabilities in both synchronous and asynchronous modes. Email is a "store and forward" technology that travels over the simple mail transport protocol (SMTP). Email messages are stored on your email server and periodically forwarded to the address of the intended recipient. Transmission can happen within the fraction of a second across a continent. Email provides a dramatic improvement over physical mail systems, especially given that there is no postage to pay for the delivery of the message. Email messages also support attachments so other documents in electronic formats can be distributed. Consumers have grown to expect "instant communication" of ideas and thoughts through email. The growing dependency on email is reflected in the ubiquity of its usage; 94 percent of all connected households use email at least once a day.

Another popular communication technology, instant messaging (IM), was introduced to the public in 1996. Instant messaging blends the strengths of synchronous and asynchronous data communication into a single application. A person using instant messaging can communicate in real time with other people. Instant messaging service providers can maintain buddy lists, instantly create private chat experiences, and have knowledge about the online presence of any buddy they have identified in their list. Instant messaging has gained great popularity, growing from zero users in 1996 to millions of users today. In 2002, 44 percent of all connected households in the United States used instant messaging at least once a day.[5] The popularity of instant messaging and email has pushed these applications into devices like the cell phone. Email and instant messaging have become part of millions of consumers' daily routines. The usage propels

---

5. Forrester Research, Inc., Consumer Survey, "Devices & Access, 2002 Online Survey," Boston: Forrester Research, Inc., 2002.

changes through all three tiers of the integrated services as follows:

- Different *device* manufacturers support email and instant messaging

- *Networks* handle the increased volume of email and instant message traffic

- *Service and application providers* build new features into email and instant messages to support customer demand

The integration of instant communication into consumers' routines encourages new features and technologies. Some data-capable mobile phones support a new technology called the multimedia messaging service (MMS). Multimedia messaging service lets mobile phone users exchange small digital images or audio clips with others. For example, a spouse will be able to send a message from his or her mobile phone with a small image, a little music, and text in order to celebrate a special occasion such as an anniversary, birthday, or graduation. One company called PacketVideo helps make mobile phones capable of receiving streamed video. New technologies such as MMS involve all three tiers for an integrated service as follows:

- Device tier: Digital video-capable mobile phone

- Network tier: Wireless digital networks that support video

- Application tier: Specialized streaming video servers that serve the video up from a hosted environment

As consumers grow to expect more from devices and services, product planners for devices and applications layer on additional capabilities that help integrate that particular service into the consumer's lifestyle.

An integrated service consists of three levels as follows: the device (such as a computer or cell phone), the network (such as the Internet or a data communication network), and the application (such as an email program or a stock quote delivery tool). Consumers adopt integrated services that enhance their lifestyle. Successful integrated services facilitate the tasks in a consumer's routine whether they involve communication, research, or entertainment. As consumers become accustomed to the advantages provided by an integrated service, the consumer begins to take the features for granted and expect more from the integrated service. For example, it's not enough to be able to simply access information on the Internet—the consumer wants only information relevant to the consumer. These changing expectations from the interactive consumer drive more innovation into new generations of the integrated service. Device, network, and application designers need to thoroughly understand how consumers integrate interactive devices into their lifestyle in order to effectively satisfy a moving target of consumer expectations. The next few chapters describe the evolution of devices, networks, and applications in response to the shifting demands of the interactive customer.

2 | Interactive Devices

An integrated service consists of devices, networks, and the applications. Devices serve as the touch point through which consumers gain access to networks and integrated services. Interactive consumers often value applications and services through the looking glass of the devices. For example, a consumer who uses email constantly depends on a computer or another Internet-enabled device to access the service. As a result, devices help sell services by providing the tangible manifestation of the service for the consumer. The evolution of customer expectations begins with the adoption of the new device and ends with new demands on the services. When consumers adopt a new device, they begin to alter their behavior to incorporate the device into their lifestyle. Buying a new cell phone introduces conversations in line at the grocery store. Subscribing to interactive television services promotes the possibility of checking email through the television. These new, learned behaviors emerge from new patterns of device and service utilization. In turn, the emergence of new learned behavior contributes to new expectations from the consumer about interactive systems in the consumer's life. The designers of interactive systems are on a perpetual treadmill of providing new integrated services in the marketplace that meet the shifting expectations of consumers.

This chapter explores the role of devices in integrated services and identifies some of the changing behaviors that are being exhibited with the adoption of these devices. By understanding the cycle of innovation and expectation, the device designer and integrated service provider can be better equipped to anticipate and respond to consumer reaction in the marketplace.

INTERACTIVE CONSUMER

The consumer electronics industry dominates the device market. From cell phones and digital cameras to game consoles and portable media players, these gadgets are devices that people hold in their hands and use on a personal basis. By 2001, approximately 56 percent of U.S. households owned a cell phone, up from 54 percent the previous year. Eight percent of households owned a PDA in 2001 compared with just 6 percent in 2000. In a 2002 consumer survey, researchers found that 18.8 percent planned to buy a video game console in the next twelve months.[1] These devices end up having certain characteristics that are consumer-oriented as opposed to business-oriented.

First, these devices tend to be trendy; there is status value ascribed to the look and feel of the devices. Technology advances and new, resource-intensive applications result in people buying updated devices on a regular basis. Most people do not walk around with a ten-year-old cell phone, or a seven-year-old game console. Both the technology and the appearance at the device level morph quickly. In most cases, devices have a utilization lifetime that ranges from six months to four years. When the device is thought of and sold as a consumer electronics device, new features and capabilities can be adopted more quickly than if the device is bundled with the service-integrated service. For example, satellite digital broadcast (DBS) networks were able to bring personal video recording capabilities to market more quickly than traditional cable television operators because the DBS

---

1. Yonish, Steve. "Benchmark May 2002 Data Overview: Covers Digital Decade Forecasts, Device Ownership, Security and Wireless," Boston: Forrester Research, Inc., May 2002.

providers treat the set-top box as a consumer device. The cable television operators view the set-top box as a terminal device that is tightly coupled with the service and therefore cannot get consumer rollout of new features and capabilities to happen as quickly.

The challenge for developers of consumer devices lies in the expectation that the device will be replaced within a relatively short period of time yet must be extremely durable. People use interactive devices. In fact, owners of interactive devices tend to use them frequently. A recent Forrester Research survey found that 35.5 percent of consumers of wireless data services sent email once a week or more. Thirty percent of users checked weather with their service.[2] While many of today's interactive devices will be collecting dust five years from now, the devices must withstand the high level of use they are going to see during that time period. To build successful devices, designers must balance the need to develop attractive user interfaces with the requirement to build a device that withstands heavy usage. It also necessitates knowing the return on investment for system infrastructure versus user interface design. For example, many people decide on what phone they want first and then decide who the service provider is going to be. As a result, phone designers spend significant research on how the user interface of the device markets to consumers to attract potential buyers up front. Phone service providers, on the other hand, focus on the reliability of the service so that once the consumer signs up, the consumer stays as a paying customer. Devices and services share a complicated relationship that is sometimes symbiotic and sometimes competitive. Devices sell services in part because the physical object makes the service tangible for the consumer. Once the consumer has adopted a new device, they can start taking advantage of the services provided via the device. The adoption of the services is what leads to new learned behaviors by the consumer. That

---

2. Yonish, Steve. "Benchmark May 2002 Data Overview: Covers Digital Decade Forecasts, Device Ownership, Security and Wireless," Boston: Forrester Research, Inc. May 2002.

relationship between device and service can be competitive as well, especially if the brand of the device subsumes the brand of the service. For example, the consumer might be more prone to remember and think positively of the manufacturer of their phone, with the brand attractively displayed on the device, than the service provider, who is the source of the unwelcome monthly bill.

ENABLING TECHNOLOGIES

The trends in the proliferation of devices have depended on key technical advances in networking. Consumers use devices to simplify or enhance everyday tasks such as keeping in touch with home or office. As a result of this use, device designers emphasize technologies that support portability, enhance presentment of richer media types, or increase reliability and durability.

Portability

As many devices become more personal in nature, they need to be able to travel and function with us wherever we go. The demand increases for devices untethered from wired connections for power and communications. What follows is a set of technologies that are meeting the increasing demands of consumers.

Portability dictates that devices need to be lighter, smaller, and powered independently for longer periods of time. Devices run on electricity and that electricity needs to have a power source. In order for devices to travel without being physically connected to a power outlet, devices rely on batteries as the source of electrical power. This leaves device designers with the two following options to meet the demands of consumers:

- Improve battery technology to hold a longer charge in a smaller and lighter package
- Reduce the power requirements of the device

While battery technology has advanced in the past twenty years, it has not had the same rate of advancement as found in microprocessor power. As a result, designers focus on creating lower power consuming devices. Traditionally, computer component designers have not concerned themselves with power consumption. Computers were housed in large boxes with internal cooling systems and connected to a power grid through a plug and a power supply. Portable computing devices change this assumption dramatically. The more electrical current a device draws, the more heat produced by the device. This heat needs to go somewhere or it can cause damage to the computing infrastructure itself or to its surroundings. Cooling systems, such as fans, draw power in order to operate. Designers of computing components focus on providing maximum processing resources with the minimal amount of power draw. For example, the microprocessor found in most PDAs is the ARM chip, which is based on the reduced instruction set chip (RISC) design. This is a processor design that typically draws much less power than traditional computer microprocessor designs (complex instruction set computer) found in earlier Intel x86 designs.

While enhancing power independence eliminates one physical, wired connection, interactive devices increasingly need to be able to communicate with a data network or other devices without having to make a physical connection. There have been significant advances in wireless networking that enable devices to communicate without needing to be physically plugged in.

There is a confusing array of wireless network technology that is being incorporated into devices. Each has their strengths and merits depending on the needs of the consumer. Different wireless networking technologies include the following:

■ Infrared communication—This technology works well over short distances and where the "line of sight" between the sending and receiving devices is clear. This technology has been used for years between remote controls and televisions. More recently, infrared communications are used for simple data transfer between PDAs, notebook computers, and phones.

▣ Bluetooth—This technology is a radio-frequency technology that is optimal for personal local area networking where "line of sight" between the sending and receiving devices may not be reliable. An example of Bluetooth technology is the ability to have a hands-free microphone and earpiece communicate with your mobile phone without the need to have tangled wires or cables.

▣ WiFi (802.11x)—There is an array of 802.11 technologies that range in bandwidth and capabilities. What is attractive about this technology is that it is an open standard that makes it cost-effective to deploy a wireless local area network (LAN). A local area network is a data communications network that enables computers, printers, and servers to all communicate. Wireless local area networks (WLAN's) enable portable devices to connect to this same network for such applications as email, printing, and file sharing. The current drawbacks in the technology involve the security of such networks and the fact that the networks are not pervasive.

▣ GSM—Wireless communications carriers are currently deploying third-generation (3G) wireless networks around the world. Most of these wireless carriers are deploying a global system for mobile communications (GSM), which covers an array of technologies and acronyms such as EDGE and GPRS. This network will provide wireless data network services anywhere that wireless phone service is available. GSM is discussed in more detail in Chapter 6.

Presentment

Another trend in devices is the need to have richer forms of presenting media over the devices. Trends in this area are dominated by advancements made in the graphics processing power within the device.

Increased usage of game consoles drives greater expectations on the graphic processing capabilities in game consoles. Game consoles host specialized graphic processing chips such as Nvidia's line of graphics integrated services. These chips provide the graphic processing power traditionally reserved for high-end simulation systems. Now the graphic processing capabilities found in Microsoft's Xbox, Sony's PlayStation, and Nintendo's GameCube create the ability for game developers to present 3D, interactive worlds in which gamers can participate.

Embedded Systems

Devices need to be able to run increasingly complex application while not requiring a full technology support staff. The software systems that come bundled on devices are known as embedded systems. Anytime you use a cell phone, play a video game, set your home's security system, or look at your schedule on a PDA, you are interacting with an embedded system.

Since embedded systems are typically interactive with their environments, they require many of the systems to be real-time in nature. Real-time systems have different requirements placed on them in contrast to older batch systems used in back-office business systems such as for billing. Embedded systems are deployed in environments where there is little technical support staff. These systems need to be highly reliable and predictable in behavior. Embedded systems also need to be very sensitive to the resources of the device they are running on. The embedded system cannot ask the device to consume power when it would be best to conserve battery life.

Embedded systems have evolved from the functions of a digital watch or calculator to full-blown operating systems functioning on PDAs. Greater functionality demands in embedded systems have resulted in more complex embedded systems while the needs of low computing resource requirements, high reliability, and real-time responsiveness remain.

The advances in enabling technology have come as a result of increased consumer expectations placed on an earlier generation of devices such as analog phones, videocassette recorders, and analog broadcast media. As consumers have adopted this earlier generation of devices, they created a new class of learned behaviors. These new learned behaviors "raise the bar" of expectations on the adopted set of devices and result in a new wave of innovation and adoption. The adoption of new interactive, networked devices and services in turn are leading to a new set of learned behaviors.

DEVICES AS GATEWAY

Devices are gateways to integrated services. As a gateway, devices become the tangible interface to a vast and intangible digital world. The types and quality of the digital services are greatly impacted by the characteristics of the device. For example, it makes little sense to have a color streaming-video service that is accessible from a black-and-white, small-screen device that has low-bandwidth access to the Internet. This section explores the primary characteristics of digital devices as gateways and discusses their implications for both the device designer and the service provider.

The primary characteristics that affect the applicability of a device as a gateway to integrated services are user interface, connectivity, and computing power. The single greatest limitation to end user adoption of device capabilities is the device's user interface. The user interface on most devices can be broken into the following two components: the presentation interface and the control interface.

The presentation interface is the primary means by which the device provides the user information and feedback. This interface is typically a combination of visual and audio feedback. For example, a game console uses the television and the lights in the console as the primary means by which to provide the consumer feedback and the digital service. Most personal computers use a monitor and speakers as the primary means of feedback. The trend in most devices is that they are becoming more personal and portable. This means that screen "real estate" is getting sparser.

The control interface is the primary means by which the consumer tells the device what function they wished performed. Most interfaces are touch-based. For example, a mouse, keyboard, and keypad are all touch-based interfaces. Since devices are becoming more personal and portable, these touch interfaces are becoming more limited.

Interactive devices are also becoming networked. As a result, the amount of data conveyed to the consumer is limited by the amount of bandwidth his or her network connection provides. Consumer networks connections can be any of the following:

- Modem connection over plain old telephone service (POTS)

- Broadband digital subscriber line (DSL) connection over local telephone connection

- Broadband connection via cable television connection

- Mobile connection from wireless carrier

All of these forms of connectivity have their strengths and weaknesses. For example, since over 90 percent of homes in the United States have a telephone connection, there is a good chance that a modem connection can be made from any of these homes. This is why the first generation of networked home computers and game consoles focused on modem connections. While modem connections can be made from many places, the connection speed, or bandwidth, is not high.

Broadband connections provide higher bandwidth for consumer use, but establishing a broadband connection has its challenges. Not all homes have cable television connections. For DSL, the local regional Bell operating company (RBOC) needs to install special network equipment to make the connection. This is sometimes a time-consuming process. In order to achieve mobile broadband access from within the home, the cable or DSL connection needs to be connected to an 802.11 or WiFi base station.

The advantage of wireless networking from wireless carriers is the ubiquitous access to data networks. The key disadvantage is the bandwidth rates. Next-generation data networks are currently being rolled out across the United States, but even these networks will not possess the bandwidth to rival cable and DSL connections into the home. Processing power and memory are the primary drivers determining the computing capabilities of any device. Richer media types require greater and greater processing capabilities in order to manipulate or present the content. There are two forms of memory on most computing devices. The first form of memory can be thought of as system memory; this is the memory that the device and application processing uses. If an application process requires more memory than what is available, there can be performance degradation or worse. The second type of memory is storage memory. This is where application binaries and content file are stored for later retrieval. If you have a large video file and no storage memory to store it, you will not be able to save that file and travel with it.

LEARNED BEHAVIORS

When consumers adopt new devices, regular use of the device will result in modified, learned behaviors as they become aware of what is possible with the new device. Most consumers buy new devices to help with traditional tasks. For example, some people buy mobile phones for safety reasons. Others buy PDAs to "get organized" in their daily routines. Through device usage, consumers begin to change their behavior around the newfound capabilities of the device. For example, while someone might have initially purchased a mobile phone for personal safety purposes, soon they find they are using it in the supermarket to get clarification from his or her spouse on a particular item to purchase.

Devices drive learned behaviors through

- Navigation—new navigation models for television, computers, and phones

- Communication—new communication models in the home and the workplace

- Organization—more information at peoples' fingertips. Some of this information is public, some is private, and all of it needs to be organized if it is to be useful

Digital devices provide a tangible interface to the integrated service. People are used to navigating the real world, but a digital world of information and content can seem boundless in comparison. People are accustomed to organizing the objects in their real world, but have begun to learn new behaviors when navigating, communicating, and organizing large amounts of information without physical constraints. Physical world analogies provide a sense or order and familiarity in using these new digital, but physical analogies might not produce the most efficient interaction with these digital objects.

Navigation

Navigation is the act of maneuvering through a medium. In the physical world, ships navigate the seas, commuters navigate through traffic, and pilots navigate the skies. Traditionally, navigating media distribution has been a relatively simple task because of the limited number of options. If you wanted to navigate from one radio or television channel to another, you simply needed to turn a dial to the appropriate channel. In a networked world with radio signals streaming from satellites and television coming into the home over broadband connections, the number of options increases dramatically. The devices that gain access to these media rich networks need to accommodate navigation challenges on an increasing scale.

A new, generalized navigation model is emerging across digital content distribution mediums. People needed to navigate music and television mediums by traveling up or down a list of channels. This was a fine method when the number of links in the chain was highly limited. When the chain has hundreds of links to choose from, navigation shifts from traveling up and down the sequence to searching for the desired programming based on known attributes.

From Stepping to Search

The move to "search" from traditional "stepping" is a powerful shift. People are modifying their behavior based on their adoption of interactive devices. Moving behavior from stepping to search places more power in the hands of the person conducting the search and raises expectations on what information will be provided. Viewers and listeners are constantly looking for greater control in their programming selection. The primary drivers for greater control are

- The increased value in people's time and

- The desire to select programming most appropriate for the context.

People conduct a search when they are looking for programming options based on particular criteria. Search engines take the person's criteria and sort through the catalog of options. The search engine then provides the person with a list of options that best match the criteria provided. Criteria could include time, programming source, topic, categorization, or key words. The following sections explore how navigation has shifted from stepping to search and the potential implications the shift has had on behavior.

Navigation on Television

In the United States, during the 1950s and 1960s, getting clear television reception was a greater challenge than programming navigation. Consumers had three major networks to choose from, with a handful of VHF channel options becoming available over time. People could keep the programming options in their own heads, because navigational assistance from the television as a device was not required. The emergence of cable and satellite television distribution changed the need for navigational assistance.

Channel options moved from the single digits in most media markets to well over a dozen options, including premium movie channels. But even this advance was a stepping stone to a world of digital television distribution. Cable and satellite systems are now capable of carrying of hundreds of channels over their digital networks. With the advancement in providing viewers greater selection comes the challenge of navigating a television medium with hundreds of channels. Simply stepping through channels one at a time as done with traditional tuners becomes a severe limitation to timely navigation and selection. The device (in this case a set-top box) needed to be augmented to assist viewers in navigating their programming options.

Devices help drive the adoption of services. The more capable the television set-top box to easily provide greater variety in television programming options is, the greater the pull for subscribers to subscribe to cable and satellite television services. To help subscribers navigate an increasing variety of programming options, the answer was an electronic programming guide (EPG). Electronic programming guides enable viewers to more easily find and select the programming they wish to watch. Rather than simply providing a listing of the channels and the ability to select them, the EPG takes "meta information" about the programming options and enables the viewer to navigate in whole new ways. For example, rather than simply saying the channel number, the title of the program, and the time that it is showing, the program can also have other meta information such as its class of programming (e.g., children, sports, and movie), whether it's premium or included in the current package, or whether it's appropriate for certain age groups (e.g., adult content). The viewer can then look at the listing in a number of different ways and choose the program that best suits him or her at the moment.

Once there is a rich catalog of programming options, detailed meta information tagged to the individual programming, and an application such as a search engine to take advantage of this meta information, a range of possibilities for navigation becomes possible. For example, viewers can look into the near future in the programming catalog and tag a particular program for future viewing. Viewers can then be notified when that program is about to begin. If viewers still prefer the "stepping" model of navigation, they can tag certain programming channels as "favorites." Then when they step through their programming options, they will only step through their favorites, thus dramatically changing the amount of channels that need to be stepped through.

Devices exist in the real world and as a result have physical constraints. For example, the primary input device for a viewer of digital cable is a television remote. While these devices have many more buttons than earlier versions, these remotes do not possess the same amount of options of a full keyboard. This is where great challenges can exist for human interface designers. As more selection becomes available, a richer navigation tool is needed. But the navigation tool can be limited by the physical reality of the input device. For this reason, already created searches are available for most EPGs in order to avoid full text entry.

In the future, it is possible that every program ever created, or any video source in operation, may be available. Such a vast catalog of possibilities will continue to place pressures on the navigational capabilities of television devices. Only if the device and the embedded systems that run on the device can make it easy for subscribers to find what they value will subscribers adopt such advanced services in the future.

Navigation through Search

Personal computers have also seen a shift from stepping through file systems to using advanced searching capabilities in order to locate desired content. Consumers will be able to purchase Internet content or advanced Web services only if they can "discover" such content and services on their terms through a device of their choosing. One of the great challenges of search engines is determining what constitutes a good search. Different search engines take varying approaches to this challenge. For example, most file system search engines index text on the different files on your computer. These files include word processing documents, spreadsheets, presentations, and Web pages. The information about all of the documents is stored in an index. The index is a look-up table matching text with the name and location of the file the text was found within. When the computer user enters some words into the search engine, the index is searched and the most relevant "hits" or matches are prioritized. The problem with this approach is that it can often produce results that are not relevant to the requestor. For example, upon entering the word *bill,* a search could produce documents containing a billing statement, a presentation with a bird's beak, and former President Bill Clinton.

An improved search takes into account the context in which the search is being made. If the search engine knows the types of things I am interested in, then the search engines can promote answers that have similar context in the documents. Finally, another search engine improvement can come from association. For example, some search engines (e.g., Google) take into account references to a document from other documents, in this case Web pages. By taking into account the relationship between documents, it is more likely that the appropriate context can be generated for producing relevant search results. In the early days of the Internet, "surfing" became quite popular. Surfing was the act of "stepping" from one site to the next from links placed on the Web pages. Eventually, directories such as Yahoo came into existence to enhance the relevance of the surfing experiences. The move from directories and surfing to search engines is the behavioral move from stepping to searching.

Navigation on Phones

Phones have traditionally been stepping devices. When you place a call, you make the call to a single address (phone number).

Traditionally, when a caller interacts with an interactive voice response system (IVR), the caller is typically stepped through options such as "for billing inquiries press 1, for account balance press 2" and so on. The wealth of data and audio content that is becoming available will force device designers to move from a "stepping" model to a "searching" model.

Just as with the television remote, the amount of device "real estate" is seriously constrained by the real-world use of the device. Voice recognition, by companies such as Nuance, is able to get around the input device constraint by enabling the input of word verbally. Once recognized, the words can be fed into a search engine or categorization engine and produce results. Hopefully, these results will be relevant to the end user. Another way of establishing context for phones is location.

Location-based services can dramatically augment a search for information from a mobile device. For example, if you want a traffic report or restaurant recommendation, by knowing the caller's location, the service knows whether to provide a traffic report for Seattle or Philadelphia without asking the caller for additional information.

Anyone who has conducted a search on the Internet knows that the value of the search relates directly to the relevancy of the search. The challenge is to extract as much context from the person conducting the search while maximizing the convenience for that person. This means the best way to help people navigate vast amounts of options in a digital world is to know as much as possible about the person and the content for which he or she is searching. This means potentially knowing the person's interests, behavior, and demographics. This also means knowing the content, attributes about the content, and how other similar individuals value that content. As one can see, this very quickly gets close to issues of privacy, profiles, and questions about consumer monitoring.

One example of a company that uses these techniques to try to maximize the benefits to their customers is Amazon.com. Amazon lets their consumers know how other consumers feel about products, provides "purchase circles" for like-minded customers, and is able to make recommendations based on past purchases and product ratings. When there is a vast amount of options to choose from, the device from which you are navigating needs to assist in making it convenient to find that which the customer values. Consumers adopt value-added interactive shopping services when they can quickly and easily get value through the device they are using.

COMMUNICATION

Continued advances in digital networks and consumer electronics have made it cost-effective for people to communicate across an increasingly diverse set of applications. As a result, the explosion in devices and means by which to communicate has lead to a more diverse set of new, learned behaviors for people communicating with one another. Different people have always had preferences in the way that they communicate. Some people express themselves best in the written word. Some people prefer meetings. Other people may prefer voice communications. The adoption of new communication devices has led to the people buying new classes of data communication services ranging from mobile email to online presentation services. This section explores some of the diverse devices and modes of communication and the different communication cultures they support.

Personal Communications

People communicate by the written word and the spoken word. Advances in digital devices and communication networks change the synchronous/asynchronous aspects of these forms of communication.

Traditionally, the written word has been an asynchronous form of communication. In other words, the two parties that were communicating did not need to be interacting in real time with one another. When someone wrote a letter, the content of the letter was stored on a piece of paper. The sender and the receiver did not need to synchronize their activities in real time in order for communication to take place.

On the other hand, the spoken word (before voicemail) is a synchronous form of communication. When two people want to talk, they need to schedule a time when they can be on the phone together at the same time in order for the communication to take place. Meetings and presentations were even a stronger form of synchronous activity because the two parties needed to coordinate the time and place.

Digital networks have enabled the written word to take the form of asynchronous and synchronous communications while the spoken word can now be done asynchronously via voicemail, and meetings no longer require physical synchronization. This enables work cultures to gravitate to the styles of communication that are most efficient and effective. Devices are becoming increasingly capable of handling diverse communication modes. For example, most mobile phones can now handle synchronous voice communications, interact with asynchronous voicemail systems, and can send and receive text messages that are synchronous (instant messaging) and asynchronous (short message service).

Asynchronous Voice

In many sales- and service-oriented cultures, the phone rules. Voicemail cultures predominate where a personal relationship is needed, but synchronous communications are not always possible. As a result of more capable devices and back-end systems, professionals who prefer voicemail can effectively move through their voicemail boxes, schedule and organize their call activity, and use the personal touch of voice to convey meaning beyond the literal definitions of the words spoken.

Asynchronous Text

While a sales professional may look forward to a full voicemail box, a software engineer may dread it. The ambiguity of the spoken word that makes the sales or service professional more productive hinders the level of specificity needed by the technical professional. As a result, technical cultures gravitate to the world of email. Email boxes can be flooded in these companies as specifications, technical assistance, and design concepts are communicated from one individual to another. The growth of Web-enabled phones and Palm Pilots (2.4 million users by the end of 2000)[3] encourages the growth of electronic communication. SMS is probably one of the greatest examples of consumers adopting a device and creating a new, learned behavior as a result of becoming familiar with the capabilities of the device over time. SMS is the ability to send short (110-character) messages from one mobile phone to another. Once carriers in Europe established the ability to send such messages between each other, there was an explosion in the amount of messaging traffic. In a 2002 European consumer survey, 14 percent of respondents claimed to send SMS from their mobile phone a couple of times per day while 15 percent of respondents said they sent messages a couple of times per week.[4]

Synchronous Text

But some people also require synchronous, or near-synchronous, communications. The Research in Motion Blackberry device provides this audience with a device that could send messages between

---

3. Gluck, Marissa, and Nikki Lewis, Ari Mayerfield, Adrienne Piras, Claudine Singer, Joe Laszlo, Michael May, Seamus McAteer. "Interactive Advertising on Post-PC Platforms: Emphasizing Modal Marketing," New York: Jupitermedia Research, January 22, 2001.
4. Jackson, Paul. "Finding New Uses for SMS," Boston: Forrester Research, Inc., June 26, 2002.

devices quickly and easily. Many others have found an answer in instant messaging. IM is an application that enables people to share correspondence in near real time. These written conversations can go on between two people or many. IM can also be performed from a number of networked devices. For example, AOL's Instant Messenger (AIM) or Microsoft's Instant Messenger can be used from a desktop computer, a laptop computer, networked PDA, or data-capable mobile phone. As more devices become capable of supporting services like instant messaging, people will establish new behaviors and demands for increased capabilities on such devices and services.

Meeting across Locations

Some professions such as consulting services, marketing communications, and creative design often require meetings in order to be truly effective. In these meetings, people are working together to communicate ideas, problems, and solutions. The use of voice, presentation materials, and whiteboards has traditionally meant that people needed to coordinate time and place in order to conduct a meeting.

Cheaper, digital video conferencing and Web-based presentation tools such as WebEx are changing the location coordination requirements for such meetings. Digital cameras can be connected to the Universal Serial Bus (USB) port on a personal computer. The digital images from the cameras can then be streamed to client software of the participant's personal computers. The presence of a relatively cheap device, such as a USB-connected camera, opens up a new class of video conferencing traditionally reserved from very expensive conference room setups.

Web conferencing extends the capabilities of the common Web browser on a personal computer to show presentations while simultaneously conducting a traditional conference call. As a result of this new capability, the way a person conducts a Web conferencing presentation is different than the way they would conduct a physical meeting or a traditional conference call. For example, the person presenting can receive questions in text from the audience without interrupting the flow of the presentation for the rest of the audience. Whether it is video or Web conferencing, these new forms of meetings and the new behaviors that result from the meetings arise from the availability of devices like networked PCs. Devices make integrated services possible for people to adopt.

Unified Messaging

Mid-sized to large companies require many functions under one virtual roof. Bridging solutions allows different areas of the company to operate within their own communication cultures. These bridging solutions enable one, optimized communication culture to interact with another communication culture via the devices of their choice. Unified messaging from companies such as Comverse enables professionals to gain access to their communications through the device that best accommodates them. For example, voicemail can be converted to email and read from a personal computer. Unified messaging can also take email and convert it into voicemail to be heard from a mobile phone. The challenge being met in the workplace today is putting the best synchronous and asynchronous communication systems that interface with the person's preferred device in place. Devices, such as mobile phones and wireless PDAs, are becoming convergence points for different modes of communication. The greater the capability of the devices, the richer the array of communication services that will be able to be accessible from these devices.

ORGANIZATION

Digital networks and devices change our notion of organization from dealing with static objects to dynamic objects. Organization for digital networks and devices is much more about managing flows of information than managing traditional objects. Increasing expectations are being placed upon digital devices to receive, organize, and publish digital content in many different forms.

Devices perform a number of functions with respect to organizing information flows. First, devices can store information. In some cases, the device stores the information locally. In others, the device serves as an access point to information.

Second, devices provide people with the ability to manage information flows. For example, people can define rules that determine the fate of the information flowing to the device. Some of these rules exist at the device while in other instances they reside on a server that the device interacts with. In either case, a person can establish criteria that indicate if the information has particular attributes, and then the user can determine what specific actions should be taken with the information. For example, many cell phones now make it possible to determine if a call is coming from a particular person on the phone's address list and then use a different ring tone to signal that call.

Not all information flows will be wanted. For example, unwanted email from direct marketers, or "spam," can be filtered and deleted at the server whether you are accessing your email from a PDA, mobile phone, or a notebook personal computer.

Finally, much of the information stored on devices should be actionable. For example, it is possible to directly make a call from the contact information stored in the phone's electronic address book.

As devices provide greater capabilities with respect to filtering, storing, and acting upon information flows, application providers can offer new services to meet consumers' increasing expectations.

Devices provide a tangible touch point for an integrated service. Consumers often associate an integrated service, such as instant messaging, with the device that displays the user interface to access the service (such as a cell phone). As a result, device designers must be especially cognizant of the relationship between consumer usage of the application, network tiers of the integrated service, and the device support for the consumer's behaviors. Factors such as the user interface, connectivity, and computing power of the device directly impact how well the device fulfills consumer expectations. Consumers learn interactive behavior through the device, which serves as the physical user interface for an integrated service. However, a successful integrated service consists of more than just the device. A successful integrated service results from a seamless combination of a device's capabilities, a network's capacity, and the application's service. Success comes from how willingly and easily the consumer integrates the integrated service into his or her lifestyle. The next two chapters explore how consumer expectations impact the audio and visual capabilities in an integrated service.

Interactive Audio

Sound is one of the foundations of human interaction. It serves as the conduit for free speech, conveys the emotional appeal in music, and most importantly, is the most commonly used vehicle for interpersonal communication. Sound in technology provides users with the ability to control how, when, and where the user hears and responds to other people as well as systems. Peoples' desire to interact by way of sound and to manipulate sounds can be seen in the rapid adoption by mainstream consumers of the telephone, tape recorder, audio mixing boards, and the CB radio. Digital, interactive networks and the devices that connect to them will provide the next generation of consumers with even greater personal control over the power of sound.

This chapter explores three ways in which consumers' expectations and uses of sound impact the evolution of digital networks. First, we take a look at how digital networks evolved from communication networks. Then we examine how digital networks change and extend how consumers buy and use music. Finally, we explore the services that sit on top of the digital networks to help consumers use the power of voice to drive device behavior. After reading this chapter, you should have a good understanding of the following topics:

- How sound has evolved through interactive technologies

- How consumers have responded to the evolution of interactive sound

▣ How the evolution of digital networks help create a market-place that address the needs of the interactive consumer

Let's start by taking a look at how sound has evolved in computers.

EVOLUTION OF AUDIO IN COMPUTING

Sound did not play a significant role in the evolution of the PC. The visual element dominated the PC revolution. A picture does not convey the same feeling as does talking with a loved one or listening to music. Audio conveys an emotional impact by inciting individual reactions based on the sound.

In personal computing, audio has been relegated to the role of *complementing* the visual experience. Often, software and device developers use sound to communicate a negative message, such as a user's error. Sound provided user-interface feedback such as alert beeps, which told the user that an incorrect key was pressed or a limit was reached in the software. The workplace settings in which personal computers were first used did not contribute to the rapid development of audio. Spreadsheet computations and desktop publishing do not require audio components. Software developers determined that limiting sound to a beep alerting the user to a wrong formula seemed more "professional" and appropriate to the office environment.

The popularity and use of Web sites and gaming contributed the most to the exploration of audio on personal computers. Music in online advertisements and announcements on Web sites became more commonly used by media-savvy Web developers to develop a richer consumer experience on the site. Gaming pushed the limits of computer sound and graphic cards, demanding more and more power to support the audio required for increasingly sophisticated games. As a result, software developers and peripheral developers began to enhance the audio capabilities of personal computers. These audio enhancements happened rapidly. In 1995, many personal computer manufacturers still charged extra for sound cards for improved audio

capabilities. Five years later, advanced sound hardware and often multimedia authoring tools come as a standard option for a new personal
computer.

The power of the consumer's demand for better quality sound
hardware has had an impact on more than the computer industry.
Consumers with high expectations in the areas of communication
and music drove other device manufacturers to improve upon previous
generations. The first radio devices came in large boxes and focused
on amplitude-modulated (AM) signaling technology. Over the years,
people wanted high-quality sound in a more portable form. The
frequency-modulated (FM) transistor radio met both of these criteria
by improving the quality of the sound broadcast as well as enabling
portability. Today radios are ubiquitous in society. The success of
radio demonstrates that in order to be adopted by the mainstream
consumer, devices must meet consumer expectation on the quality
of sound, portability, and control and be highly cost effective for the
value provided.

Advances in enabling technologies provide consumers with the
ability to expand their options for choice in audio consumption.
These technologies enhance the role of sound in advanced, networked
devices by providing the following benefits:

- Improved format conversion from analog to digital

- Increased processing power for devices and networks

- Data networks

- User interfaces for audio consumption

ANALOG TO DIGITAL

For human beings, audio is an analog experience. Analog transmis-
sions are made up of waves traveling at different frequencies and
amplitudes. Sound travels via waves in the air which are received

by our ears. Tiny movements deep in our ears are translated into sound by our brain. Traditional telecommunication networks such as the telephone or radio networks convert the frequencies and amplitudes of airwaves into electromagnetic wave equivalents and then send these electromagnetic wave equivalents over wires or through the air to devices on the receiving end. The receiving devices convert the electromagnetic waves back into airwaves for our ears to hear.

In order to carry the audio waves over distances, designated channels need to be created to deliver the audio signal. For radio, a particular electromagnetic wave frequency is designated to a radio station for broadcasting. The consumer tunes his or her radio to receive that frequency. For phones, a designated circuit over a switched network creates the connection between the two phones. The problem with both of these approaches is that the amount of information (in this case, audio) that can be sent over the channel or circuit is not optimized. This is wasteful and ultimately makes the networks costly to support millions of consumers.

Sound can be converted from an audio format to a digital format, which represents the frequencies and amplitudes as series of electronic ones and zeros. A digital format enables audio delivery over networks that do not require a designated channel or circuit. Combine the ability to share channels and circuits with advances in digital compression technologies and you gain bandwidth. Why is this important to the consumer? Because it enables audio to be moved over networks in a more robust way, with higher quality sound. You can send more audio over the same resource (the electromagnetic frequency or wire). Digital formats make communication networks cheaper in the long run, thus enabling lower prices to be passed on to the consumer in a competitive marketplace. This environment, in turn, provides a viable distribution channel for the creators of new and converted audio content. The availability of the distribution channel and its supporting technology introduces new opportunity for content as well as difficult questions about legally protecting content. Ultimately, consumer adoption of audio content and supporting devices drives a greater demand for both the content itself and audio functionality in devices.

DATA NETWORKS

Traditionally, telecommunications services have traveled over switch-based networks (also called switched networks). A designated channel had to be created between the originator of the sound signal and the recipient of the sound signal. These networks were optimized for service delivery, whereas other distribution models, such as broadcast or performance models, were not. Broadcast and performance models have been supported through broadcast networks such as radio and television, but, as we've discussed, the amount of interactivity that can be attained through these broadcast-centric networks is highly limited.

Digital networks make connections in a different way. Data are broken up into a set of packets. Each packet has an address for where it needs to go. The packets are then sent into the network and go through routers that look at the address and send the message on in the network. The network is extremely robust, since the packets can take multiple paths to reach their destination. If there is network congestion (high call volume) in one part of the network, the packets can be quickly sent through other routers to reach their destination.

The Internet brought about a new type of network based on digital information. A digital-based network takes the sound (in digital form), cuts it up into a set of packets, and routes the packets across the network to the recipient's network address. Digitally based networks offer two primary benefits for the distribution of sound. First, digitally based networks require fewer resources than a switched network, thus bringing down the cost for sending sound over the network. It is potentially far cheaper for a network operator to route phone calls this way than by relying on a traditional switched network to carry the call traffic. Traditional switched networks tie up circuits until the call is finished, thus not maximizing the bandwidth of the line. In this way, digital networks bring down the cost of handling a minute of voice. Second, a digitally based network is a two-way network. A two-way network enables a much richer interaction between the sender and the receiver of the sound than what is currently available over traditional broadcast networks. These new efficiencies in transmitting sound cut down the costs of audio delivery and open the door for more resource-intensive delivery of audio, such as with Web-casting radio or live performances.

New Audio in Networks

Digital formats, devices, and networks help address users' demand for the highest quality of sound at the best value. Digital format exceeds analog format in cost-effectiveness and capabilities. Network technology has also made significant leaps, with digital networks beginning to surpass traditional circuit switched networks in cost, reliability, and flexibility. But consumers often don't equate the background technology, like digital networks, with the experience; rather, it's the device designs that respond to the users' demands for portability, user control, and cost effectiveness. Devices such as phones have identities rooted in the audio experience. Visual interfaces might augment phones and portable music devices, but the roots of these devices remain grounded in the audio experience. Consumers will not tolerate the core identity of these devices being compromised. If the consumer's perceived identity for a device is primarily a phone, no matter how many bells and whistles are added to the device, the consumer will demand that it still be a top-notch phone. The combined use of digital networks for superior audio transmission with an appealing, cost-effective, and user-friendly delivery system explains why a device such as the cell phone has almost reached the same level of ubiquity as the radio in today's society.

The manner in which sound is consumed greatly impacts consumers' expectations of the quality of the audio experience. A person might not expect hi-fidelity sound from an AM radio broadcast but would expect it from a digitally formatted CD played on an expensive sound system at home.

Sound in Daily Routines

Sound is consumed in four primary ways as follows:

1. As a *service* used to complete a task, such as wireless phone service

2. As a *commodity* to be bought, such as a music CD

3. In a *broadcast* format, such as a radio show

4. Through a live *performance* or other direct interaction

Telecommunications is an example of how sound is consumed as a service. A network operator such as AT&T or Sprint provides a distribution network for the sound to be delivered. The operator's network connects to end devices (phones) that subscribers use to access the sound services. The consumer typically compensates the network operator by paying a base rate and then paying incremental fees above that base rate calculated by usage. Rarely is it the case that a network operator owns the entire network the consumer is utilizing, especially over great distances. For example, the price for a long-distance phone call gets split among all the network operators involved in placing the call (local and/or long-distance operator). The fragmentation of a single call over multiple service networks has driven a trend to consolidate networks in the telecommunications industry. Network operators want to keep the costs of such calls within their own networks and not be forced to share the revenue from the call.

Consumers do not particularly care which network operator handles the call. What they do care about is low cost, increasingly high levels of sound quality, always-accessible networks, and quickly resolved issues, no matter what the cost might be to the network operator. The expectation around a service like telecommunications differs greatly from that of buying a retail product. When the warranty is up on the product, the retailer and manufacturer no longer have a relationship with the consumer. With a service, the service provider always has a relationship with the consumer as long as the consumer is a customer. As a result, the service might be more inclined to maintain a high level of quality to extend the lifetime of the customer account.

Consumer demand and loyalty drive companies that provide audio as a service. The three metrics most often used by a network provider are as follows:

- The average revenue per subscriber, including the ability of the provider to up-sell the subscriber into new services

- The support and operations cost per subscriber, which ties directly back to the customer service relationship with the customer

- The retention rate of the subscriber base, often described as the *churn rate* (the percentage of customers lost annually)

It is impossible for the network operator to be profitable if the average cost per subscriber is greater than the average revenue per subscriber. As a result, network operators must be extremely sensitive to customer expectations for quality and service, as well as streamlining customer support costs and simplicity in operations. Network operators that ignore customer expectations around audio and concentrate solely on reducing the cost of the customer for network operations see the negative impact on their churn rate. Keeping churn rates low is extremely important to a network operator. If it costs a network operator $240 to acquire a new subscriber through marketing and promotional costs and the network operator is charging $20 per month, it will take a full year just for the network operator to recoup the acquisition costs. If the subscriber cancels his or her subscription after six months, the network operator loses money.

AUDIO AS RETAIL COMMODITY

Consumers' expectations and use of audio as a commodity have significantly affected how people interact with commercial music. When a consumer buys a CD or a cassette from a traditional retail channel, the consumer expects to own the CD or cassette. The reality is that the consumer has purchased *a personal use license*. A personal use license means that the consumer can play the CD or cassette, make backups, or give the CD away as a gift. A personal use license prohibits the owner from making copies of the CD or cassette and then selling or giving away those copies to others. Even making a mixed tape with songs from the CD is considered piracy by the music industry. A potential loophole in the personal use license is sharing. If I lend my CD to a friend while I borrow theirs in exchange, then technically we are not breaking the personal use license.

This tension between the consumer and music industry's definition of ownership of the audio has spawned the growing use of song-swapping services on the Internet. The song-swapping services, initially led by Napster in the late 1990s, argue that the services simply allow users to share music and is therefore not in violation of the personal use license. The tremendous popularity of the song-swapping services demonstrates how a consumer expectation (the ability to exchange and share music) affects the pattern of audio consumption. In addition, the availability of songs on the personal computer has contributed to the evolution of the computer from a productivity tool to a multimedia center. This evolution raises huge issues about ownership, piracy, and copyrights for content, which is outside this discussion. From a device perspective, however, online music demonstrates how consumer usage transforms or at least expands the purpose of a device.

AUDIO IN BROADCAST FORMAT

Audio in broadcast format satisfies the consumer expectation that high-quality audio is always available and easily accessible through a standard device. Broadcast models, such as radio, are primarily supported through advertising revenues. As a result, the broadcaster targets the ears and minds of the maximum number of listeners in a demographic that is attractive to the buyers of advertising.

The radio broadcast model has downsides for both the consumer and the radio broadcaster. First, the consumer has no control over the playlist for the radio station—listeners may not hear the exact song they want when they want. Second, if listeners travel outside of the broadcast range of the radio station, they can't access preferred disk jockeys. Finally, listeners must spend some portion of their listening time on advertisements that were not their intention to listen to in the first place. The broadcaster on the other hand is completely dependent on ad revenue. Despite fixed costs for the radio production, the broadcaster might have highly variable revenue from advertising.

While radio provides a cost-effective means to consume audio, it fails to provide the consumer with *interactive choices*—such as locality of radio broadcast or control over playlist. Internet-based radio broadcasting attempts to address the listener's mobility limitation by integrated service live radio programs via the Web. Listeners can "tune in" by going to Web sites and listen to broadcasts in different regions of the country or even international broadcasts. This new level of interactivity in radio extends the reach of the radio broadcast by providing more choice to the listener. In addition, advertisers for radio programs broadcast simultaneously on local radio and the Web have a far greater potential reach than through local radio alone.

PERFORMANCE

The final area to explore for how people consume sound is performance, typically live performance such as concerts. In the case of performance, the listener controls the selection of the content. After all, the listener buys a ticket for a performance to be played at a particular place and at a particular time. On the other hand, the listener has no influence over the forum for the performance or the time that the performance is launched. New technologies like Web-casting allow concerts to be broadcast over the Internet. Best consumed over broadband connections, this new form of media combines audio and video to project a concert onto the listener's personal computer. Not only can the listener control who to hear but also when and how to view the performance. As with radio, sponsors of a Web-cast performance have the ability to reach far more potential buyers than with a local showing.

While Web-casting performance introduces new opportunities for the listener to control the consumption of audio, it remains primarily a novelty for mainstream performances. Web-casting requires that listeners have a high-speed connection or risk watching and listening to media interrupted by stops and starts in the transmission. In addition, many listeners continue to prefer the ambiance of attending a live performance. New technologies introduce more interactive possibilities for listeners but must provide a significant-enough advantage (such as cost or selection) over traditional audio to replace or supplement an established behavior.

CHANNELS IN CONFLICT?

Diverse channels of sound consumption are not necessarily cannibalistic—that is, a listener can tune in on an Internet broadcast on the computer and later turn on the radio in the car. Moreover, the music industry exploits different forms of retail, broadcast, and performance models today. The consumer's drive toward greater interactivity creates tremendous opportunity for service providers to meet the demand. The new trend toward consumer choice in consumption of audio also encounters tremendous resistance from established industries that are optimized for fulfilling consumer demand through existing channels. Only the target market itself can overcome the barriers from the established industries.

Music consumers, especially younger generations, who spend more time on the computer, can support the new channels of distribution and force the established industries to accommodate the shift. Many consumers prefer to consume their music via an online swapping service rather than through the traditional retail channel. Music labels have no experience in being a network operator. The music industry built its profits and successes on the traditional method of selling sound through the physical retail model and is struggling to understand how to monetize the electronic distribution of music. The music industry continues to fight to own the service model for music consumption. The music industry prefers to augment the existing highly optimized distribution channel rather than endanger a sales channel that produces billions of dollars of revenue to everyone in the value chain.

Device manufacturers produce a growing selection of devices tailored for the electronic delivery of music, such as MP3 players. As more users choose the mobility and selection provided by online music services, the traditional retail channel for music may find itself in a challenging battle for the interactive consumer.

The wireless communications industry also faces the challenge in a collision of business models. Consumers continue to shift toward making wireless carrier decisions based on the type of phone offered. The importance of the phone in that consumer decision shifts the power in the supply chain from the network operator to the phone manufacturer. Network operators resist the greater role that the phone manufacturers play in a purchase. The network operator spends billions on developing networks and part of that return comes in brand recognition by the consumer. Wireless carriers continue to try to distinguish their own brands, differentiate on new digital services, and consolidate networks in order to optimize their competitive cost structures. However, if phone manufacturer brands, such as Nokia, become more important to the consumer than the network provider brand, the phone device provider essentially gates the availability and use of new digital services offered by the network provider. The phone manufacturer can choose to only take advantage of common capabilities across varying wireless carriers, leaving the network provider with little used, yet operationally expensive new digital services. The consumer's demand for choice of device drives the conflict between the phone manufacturers' retail-oriented model and the wireless carriers' service-oriented model.

NETWORKED VOICE

Families and friends have always had the need to be interconnected by voice. Voice transcends location and brings diverse and dispersed communities together. The dramatic shift in network from analog signals to switched circuit networks to digital signals in packet-routed networks offers dramatic advantages to consumers. While the consumer does not value the differences of the technical delivery mechanism, consumers do value enhanced quality and services. What advantages are to be gained from digitizing sound and having it travel over new networks?

The new digital networks provide the following benefits to end consumers:

- *Flexibility*—The new digital wireless networks enable whole new classes of communication-based applications to cross the gap between the world of text-based communication and voice-based communication.

▣ *Quality*—Wireless digital networks have stronger signal recognition characteristics that make sound quality dramatically better than that of traditional analog technology.

▣ *Cost-effectiveness*—Converting analog voice into digital data applies the advances in processing power and compression technologies. As a result, more information can flow over a common infrastructure as opposed to opening a designated channel through a switched network.

▣ *Pricing*—Digital data networks provide efficiencies in pricing for existing phone operators or new Internet protocol- (IP) based operators like Net2Phone which in turn can be passed along to the consumer.

Voice over Internet Protocol

Voice over IP (VoIP) takes advantage of packet-based networks to offer new options for using audio as communication. Traditionally, the only companies that could provide consumers with local telephone service were RBOCs. VoIP offers the interactive consumer more options. For example, cable television providers are converting their networks to provide a digital broadband connection into the home through the coaxial cable that connects to a cable television box. Through this cable television connection, you can now receive digital telephone service for local and long-distance calling. Traditional RBOCs who also provide broadband services are also looking to switch some of their entire infrastructure to IP-based networks in order to reduce costs. For example, Qwest, a regional Bell operating company, is in the process of converting its entire telecommunications network to a digital IP-based network.

Consumers will take advantage of the fact that VoIP will bring lower telecommunication costs. All new services can be layered onto the digital telephone service. Examples of these services include advanced voicemail, unified messaging, caller ID services, and advanced conference calling—all audio choices offered to the interactive consumer. As telecommunication charges continue to come down in cost, entrepreneurs will find new services that are now cost-effective to deploy to consumers via existing telecommunication networks or IP-based providers. These new services may involve content subscription services such as music services, audio books, or educational content.

Digital Wireless Networks

The wireless phone has had rapid consumer adoption in both domestic and international markets. By the end of 2001, 58.7 million U.S. households owned a cell phone, approximately 56 percent of U.S. households.[1] In Europe, a full 71 percent of all consumers own and use mobile phones, with ownership as high as 86 percent in some European countries like Finland.[2] Earlier, we discussed how consumers view the value of services through the capabilities of the devices. It has never been truer than with mobile phones. Logically, the quality and reliability of the network is extremely important. However, the quality and reliability of the service (or lack thereof) more often leads to consumers *abandoning* a carrier rather than being the compelling reason for buying the service in the first place. The most compelling sales tools for the service itself are the physical device that represents the service: the phone. A handset with a compelling industrial design incurs much more consumer enthusiasm for selecting a particular service than do lengthy descriptions of the network behind the device.

The first mobile phone networks were cellular in nature and used analog signals traveling across the airwaves. Wireless carriers are

1. Yonish, Steve. "Benchmark May 2002 Data Overview: Covers Digital Decade Forecasts, Device Ownership, Security and Wireless," Boston: Forrester Research, Inc., May 2002.
2. Jackson, Paul. "Consumer Devices & Services Europe April 2002 Data Overview: Covers PCs, Net Access, Mobiles, iDTV, And Brands," Boston: Forrestor Research, Inc., April 2002.

moving to digital networks as quickly as possible. Digital networks let wireless carriers offer improved sound quality, reduce network costs, and layer additional services and capabilities. The migration from analog to digital will take time. If cellular networks were first generation, and initial digital networks were second generation, it will be the third generation (3G) of wireless network technology, as depicted in Figure 3-1, that gives users a compelling blend of data and voice services over higher bandwidth networks.

Voice Interfaces

One of the great challenges facing the designers of digital devices is to pack greater and greater functionality into smaller and smaller devices. This creates a user-interface dilemma. How are people going to access the increasing power in the device through a more limited physical user interface? The answer may lie with the power of voice interfaces.

User interfaces are the means by which people command an application or device to do their bidding. On a phone, you dial a number to place a call. On a calculator, you punch numbered keys to make calculations. A voice interface enables a person to command a device through his or her voice. Voice interfaces can not only enable people to gain access to functionality from their devices (such as voicemail commands from their phone) but can also reduce costs in customer service and support.

Most applications used on personal computers provide visual information on the screen and respond to the user from a touch-based interface such as a keyboard or mouse. This type of interface works well at a desktop, where you have a keyboard, a mouse, and a monitor, but it becomes problematic when you move to new, networked devices. Television remote controls and mobile phones have keypads but not full keyboards. Most PDAs have touch screens, buttons, and handwriting recognition, but lack a true keyboard. As greater functionality becomes available over such devices, people must be able

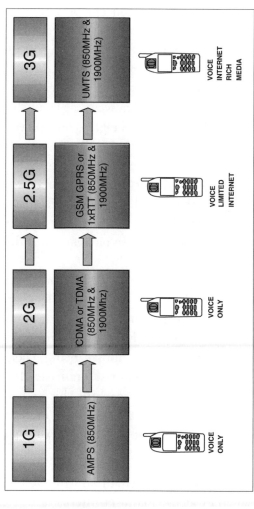

FIGURE 3-1. Evolution of Functionality through Wireless Network Generations

to interact with richer applications through a limited user interface. One way in which users will be able to interact with such applications will be with their voice rather than their fingers.

It is important that these new voice-based user interfaces be built with "affordances" in them. The concept of a perceived affordance was put forth by J. J. Gibson and then applied to computer interface design by Don Norman. Both men were trying to understand the optimal relationship between a person and a device. A perceived affordance is when a cultural constraint or convention is employed such that an end-user intuitively knows what he or she should do to gain a desired result. For example, the grips on a bicycle handle have ridges where your fingers fit nicely. Ideally, no one should need to read a manual to know how to have a device perform a desired action. Instruction should be self-evident through a perceived affordance in the user interface such that, in this case, a voice-based application could call a person from the address book if the person's name is stated. As a result, there is no need to navigate an address book from a tiny phone user interface.

It is important for the designers of these voice user interfaces to stay within the expectations of today's users. If a user interface is too anthropomorphic in nature, the user's expectations typically rise above a level that can be satisfied by the application. When a person thinks they are interacting with a human being, their expectations about the quality of the interaction rise dramatically. If the person believes he or she is talking to a machine, his or her expectations about the flexibility of the interaction go down dramatically.

Factors driving devices and applications toward voice interfaces include the following:

- Many devices need to be small and portable, thus limiting the visual and touch-based user interfaces.

- Devices must be a cost-effective way to interact with consumers, thus bringing costs into alignment with what consumers can afford.

◧ Devices need to provide a common user interface for applications across multiple voice-enabled devices.

◧ Devices need to be accessible by handicapped users whose sole form of navigation may be through the voice.

Interactive Voice Response Systems

Most of us have experienced an IVR system. Many customer support systems today have the user navigate through menus by pushing the correct buttons to route them. You navigate many of these systems by speaking the option number you wish.

As services become more integrated, the expectations around customer care and support go up dramatically. It costs companies a significant amount of money to hire, train, and retain skilled customer support professionals. As integrated services get more complex, many customer support professionals need to become more specialized in their area of support expertise. IVR systems enable companies to reduce the amount of customer support professionals needed or to more efficiently route support incidents to the most skilled person to handle the request. When companies can reduce their operating costs, it can translate into reduced costs to the consumer if there is a competitive environment for the services.

Many IVR systems are highly limited in the input that the system can handle from the person at the other end of the phone. They are not very flexible at understanding anything beyond the commands the system is expecting.

Natural language interfaces provide a much more flexible means for a person to interact with a system. Rather than simply stating "one" the person can use references like "the first one" or "I'll take the one before last." With advanced artificial intelligence and faster processors, technologists are now bringing production-quality natural language interfaces to market. People give commands or feedback with their own words. Natural language interfaces take into account context and voice recognition capabilities in order. One application for more flexible voice commands is voice portals.

Voice Portals

Voice portals are similar to Web-based portals in that they are a directory of content and applications where the portal provides navigational support for getting to the content and applications. Applications and content can include news, weather, sports, traffic, or travel information. Imagine going to Yahoo, but navigating the Yahoo directory with your voice rather than with your mouse.

Voice portals can be an attractive service to customers of wireless digital networks. For example, a voice portal named TellMe provides mobile phone users with information about the weather at a destination city and traffic conditions to the airport.

Wireless carriers make money on voice portals by charging you for the minutes you use when listening to the portal. The voice portal makes money either by being compensated by the wireless carrier as a value-added service or through advertising on the voice portal itself.

Voice Interfaces in the Future

There remain many significant challenges to making voice interfaces a preferred user interface for most people. The technology behind voice as a navigational tool needs to continue to improve so the application can understand different accents and languages. Voice application design needs to advance as an engineering discipline so the correct device behavior arises from the words said in context and perceived affordances are well understood. Finally, richer and richer applications that take advantage of the technology must be deployed.

Even with these issues to overcome, the ubiquity of voice interfaces appears well assured simply due to the demands of interactivity on small devices. Devices and services continue to get more complex while continuing to have limited physical user interfaces. Service operators continue to need to control their customer support costs. And finally, in a world where most people have not used a computer, but voices have always been used, the eventual ubiquity of devices and service will necessitate voice interfaces in order to assure consumer adoption.

NETWORKED MUSIC

Consumers take advantage of the new digital networks to enhance the options of sharing and consuming music. As discussed earlier, the traditional channel of music retail consists of moving CDs and cassettes through physical retail stores. This model restricts consumer choice to the selection of titles confined in the retail shelf space. The consumer also adheres the retail hours of the store for making music purchases.

Networked music sharing services give consumers access to a very large catalog of titles. In addition, the consumers can access the catalog anytime and wherever they are connected to the network (such as their dorm room). The catalog often includes songs that would not be traditionally sold through a retail channel because the music label might consider the audience too "niche" to waste precious retail space. Networked music also provides the consumer with the ability to download the song to a portable device such as an MP3 player.

The new flexibility in networked music introduces new consumer expectations. For example, consumers expect a greater selection of music to choose from, based on the large catalogs accessible through song swapping on the Internet. Consumers also expect the ability to gain access to the music anytime and from any networked device. Since the consumer is obtaining music from a service operator versus the traditional retail channel, the consumer has increasing customer support demands from the operator. The challenge for the service provider lies in recouping costs for providing and servicing the music network over time, much like the phone network operator.

Networked music services take advantage of peer-to-peer networking. Peer-to-peer networking enables one person on a personal computer to quickly and easily share files with another person on a personal computer. Peer-to-peer networking works equally well for music files and for other media types as well, such as video.

The first step in an online music network is making music available in a universally used digital music format. The most common format used today is MP3. A person takes their favorite CD, places it in the CD drive of their personal computer, and then uses a software program called a "ripper" to copy and convert the music from the CD into an MP3 file on their personal computer. Once on the personal computer, the MP3 files can be played in the computer, downloaded to a portable MP3 player, or shared in a peer-to-peer file-sharing network.

The peer-to-peer file-sharing network enables the broad distribution and sharing of music files over the Internet. A person can download an application that allows them to connect to a network. The file-sharing network creates a large, searchable directory of the songs across all the personal computers and servers connected to the network. All a user needs to do is enter a song title or artist's name and he or she will receive a list of available MP3 files. The MP3 file can then be selected and downloaded for local playing or further downloading to a portable MP3 player.

The primary problem for the peer-to-peer file-sharing networks lies in the lack of an economic model that compensates the music label and the artist. When copies are made and distributed without permission or compensation to the music label or artist, it is considered piracy by the music industry.

The music industry argues that creativity will not flourish if creativity is not compensated. The next generation of networked music services must try to address this need. It will be a daunting task. Since the music networks are provided as a service, subscribers bring the enhanced expectations that come with a subscription relationship.

New expectations include size of selection, quality of service, and exceptional customer care and support. At the same time, music services try to combat piracy through technologies like digital rights management (DRM).

Digital Rights Management

Digital rights management (DRM) is an enforcement technology that enables the buyer of the music to consume the music within the scope of the personal use license. The goal of DRM is to ensure that content can only be used by authorized recipients. Typically, the entity producing the music file tags the file with permissions such as how many times the song can be played, on what devices it can be played, and whether the song can be copied. The music player on the computer or the device knows how to read these permissions and provides the person playing the music the options available based on the distribution rights. For example, Microsoft Corporation's DRM technology, Windows Media Rights Manager, provides content distributors with a tool that defines rules for usage and "locks" digital media files with a license key. The content's business rules can include the number of times the file can be played, whether the file can be burned on a CD-ROM, the license start and expiration dates, and devices on which the media can be played. The license itself contains the rights that govern the usage of the content. Once the file is encrypted, the content distributor distributes the file to consumers.

Figure 3-2 describes the process of accessing digitally protected media files. When the consumer attempts to play the encrypted media file, the Windows Media Player looks for the license required to unlock the content. If the license exists on the consumer's machine, the user plays the content as expected. If the user does not have a license on the machine, the user is rerouted to a license clearing house. The license clearing house issues a license by recreating the key. The clearing house then downloads the key within an encrypted license to the user's machine. The license is bound to the user's machine and cannot be shared between machines.

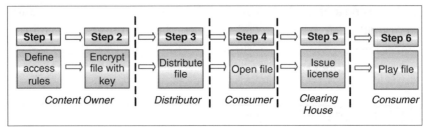

FIGURE 3-2. Microsoft's Windows Media Protection Solution

To provide flexibility in the user experience, the Windows Media Rights Manager allows content managers to deliver licenses to consumers before or after the consumer tries to play the media and also with or without consumer interaction. DRM solutions like the Windows Media Rights Manager attempt to provide content owners with a viable means of collecting revenue from content usage no matter what form of distribution—email, Web site, or any other channel.

DRM has been a long-vaunted promise for and from the music industry. There have been many industry initiatives between music labels, consumer electronic companies, and technology vendors. One such initiative is the Secure Digital Music Initiative (SDMI). The goal of the group is to create a common set of standards to enable digital rights management between devices and music services. After multiple trials, conferences, and meetings, SDMI is no closer to creating a common DRM standard for music than the other private companies that tried to develop software solutions and cross-label alliances.

Digital rights management has not yet proved successful for many reasons. First, the music labels, the consumer electronic companies, and the DRM technology companies cannot agree on a single DRM standard. Second, most DRM technologies are not "friendly" (easy to use) for the person using the technology. If the rights management for the song makes playing the song too difficult and/or time consuming for the user, the user will simply not play the song. Finally, there is a great deal of confusion and disillusionment for consumers around the standards initiative. The music industry has been working on a digital rights standard since the mid-1990s, with little or no real success. As a result, what little consumer enthusiasm for digital rights management there is is severely curbed by the uncertain future of the current solutions available.

A closely related technology to digital rights management is digital audio watermarking, which is related to the use of visual watermarks to distinguish print copies and originals. Digital audio watermarks are stamps that are placed within the digital format of the file. A music file is made up of a bunch of ones and zeros. An audio watermark is a sequence of ones and zeros that hides among the song data, but does not disrupt the quality of the song. With such a watermark it is possible to track back to the original owner for piracy enforcement purposes. If someone tries to remove the digital watermark, they land up destroying or degrading the audio quality of the song. Digital watermarking is "friendlier" to users because the consumer does not require special software on his or her computer or device to play a song. The music industry does not accept watermarking as a prevention mechanism for fraud like DRM. Given the viral nature of email and peer-to-peer music networks, it would be an expensive proposition for the labels to monitor and track every single user of the music file.

Streaming Music

Streaming audio offers an alternative to digital networks of MP3 files. Streaming audio supports subscription services-based business models, broadcast-based business models, and performance-based business models. Streaming audio does not require the large local storage requirements of file-based music networks. Because the audio is located on the server and not distributed to a client device like a computer, streaming does not have the piracy associated with file based music networks. Given these benefits, streaming audio provides the most effective balance between the needs of the consumer for inter-activity and the needs of the music industry to protect investment. Let's take a look at how streaming audio works.

In a streaming audio environment, music is first converted into a digital format that a streaming server can use. The listener has application software on his or her personal computer such as Real Networks' RealOne Player or Microsoft's Media Player. The person then selects a song. The application points to the streaming server and requests the song from the server. The streaming server breaks the song into digital packets and downloads the packets to the application on the person's personal computer. The audio does not get saved to the computer, but is "streamed" from the server to the receiving device of the listener.

The benefits for the consumer of streaming technology include the following:

- The ability to listen to a continuous broadcast of more than one song

- Large memory storage is not needed on your personal computer (as with file-based music services)

- The content provider can provide added value services like a disk jockey.

The primary disadvantage of streaming technology lies in the require-ment that the user be connected to the network in order to listen to the audio. The music is not portable such as with music files. In ad-dition, the quality of sound is limited by the user's bandwidth. The more bandwidth the user has, the better the quality of the sound. The user is at the mercy of the connection with the server. Connections can drop unexpectedly or network traffic on the server can disrupt the audio transmission.

While streaming audio introduces interesting solutions for the piracy issue in music distribution, its significant limitations on the user's mobility while listening to music and the dependency on network connections hamper its appeal to the interactive consumer. Streaming audio is a better alternative to file-based music services from the music industry's perspective. For the consumer accustomed to choice, mobility, selection, and service, the file-based music networks still provide a superior service. Only by overcoming its mobility and network limitations can streaming audio hope to earn a broad base of interactive consumers.

There has always been change in the way music is packaged and consumed. The record was displaced by the 8-track. The 8-track was displaced by cassettes. CDs have eclipsed cassettes. The Sony Walkman, and eventually the DiscMan, made music portable. It is a sure bet is that the distribution and consumption of music will continue to change. Portable MP3 players that can store hundreds of songs, a vast inventory of networked catalogs, and the universality of connecting to digital networks help pave the way for new changes by extending consumers' expectations about interactivity and audio. It is the challenge of the music industry (and music-oriented consumer electronics products) to figure out how to meet consumers' increasing expectations surrounding music while still turning a profit.

Digital networks are providing consumers with high-quality service at lower costs with increasing functionality. Consumers' expectations cannot help but rise in such an environment. One of the most interesting challenges facing the providers for networked sound will be the collision of distribution models and past and future customer expectations.

Devices sell services. In this statement lies a great challenge for wireless carriers and other network operators like music service providers. Consumers make their wireless carrier "service" decision based upon a "retail-oriented" phone decision. The result changes the balance of power between the device manufacturers and the network operators. The music industry faces an equally ambiguous future. Consumers have tried—and appreciate—unlimited selection, portability of hundreds of songs, and access when they want. The traditional retail channel dominates music sales, but the expectations created by file-swapping networks can only be met by a service integrated service. Such service integrated services will require infrastructure and customer care. This is new business operations territory for the music labels. Overcoming these challenges while fighting piracy and ensuring interoperability with device manufactures will be an all-consuming set of tasks.

Voice interfaces can provide the answer to many challenges surrounding the deployment of new digital networked services. While voice recognition technology has some problems to overcome in order to support natural language interfaces, the future appears bright. Voice interfaces can provide simpler, intuitive user interfaces for increasingly complex devices and services. Voice interfaces can bring down customer support costs. And finally, intuitive voice interfaces can help put technology into the hands of people who have never used technology before.

As is shown in the next chapter, digital networks and devices transform more than simply audio. Consumers' expectations are changing around all forms of media. One of the greatest areas of change lies in the visual experience.

Visual Evolution

Digital networks and devices change our expectations about managing and accessing visual images. Photographs capture memories, movies share rich stories, and we escape to new worlds and perform the humanly impossible via video games. As technologies emerge to give users control over visual imagery, interacting between photos, video, and televised images becomes an active engagement rather than a passive experience.

This chapter will explore three ways that digital networks change a user's visual expectations. First, we take a look at the change in consumers' expectations about how we build shared memories with digital photography and digital video. Second, we explore the evolution of television, as the viewer gains control over television content. Technologies like digital video recorders (DVRs) and video on demand have changed how we watch TV by extending the viewer's understanding of programming and control in viewing. Finally, we discuss the phenomenon that is video gaming and explore the impact of a networked gaming world. After reading this chapter, you should have a good understanding of the following topics:

- ▣ Which enabling technologies impact the evolution of visual interactive experiences

- ▣ How consumers create new learned behaviors by adopting interactive visual technologies

◘ How new visual interactive services are built on top of the next generation of digital devices and networks

Before delving into these areas, let's first take a look at the relationship between consumers and their visual experiences.

CONSUMERS AND VISUAL EXPERIENCES

We watch television, see movies, and take photographs by the millions. While people have been able to capture images and video for some time, their ability to manipulate and share their work has been limited by the costs and complexities of handling analog formats. Digital formats, devices, and networks have opened a new, empowering chapter in the capture, manipulation, and sharing of visual experiences.

Capturing images has always had the limitation of not knowing whether you are satisfied with the result at the time you take the picture. Later in the chapter, we show that people can now make determinations surrounding the image or video they just captured on site. With the use of a personal computer, images and video in digital format can now be edited or augmented to optimize the enjoyment of the visual experience. And finally, digital images and videos can be distributed and shared over digital networks in ways that guarantee the quality of the visual experience.

ENABLING VISUAL TECHNOLOGIES

One of the reasons that consumer expectations have changed about visual imagery involves the advances in video technologies for networked devices. These trends include the following:

◘ Format conversion

■ Increased processing power

■ Digitally based networks

Format Conversion: Analog to Digital

The shift from analog formats to digital formats is as profound in the realm of the visual as it is for sound. For human beings, visual experiences are analog experiences. Light travels to the eye as electromagnetic waves. These electromagnetic waves travel at different frequencies, thereby producing different colors. Visual experiences travel at the frequencies of visible light. For traditional photography, the process of capturing an image is an analog, chemical process. When you watch broadcast television, video is being sent by an electromagnetic signal to your television antenna. Your television then converts the desired frequencies or channels into a visual image that it projects on your screen. VHS tape is simply magnetic tape that is storing an electromagnetic signal that the VCR feeds the television, which then converts it to a visual signal.

Transforming analog signals into a representative series of ones and zeroes constitutes the act of digitally converting visual images and video into digital formats. Because of the size of digital formats, compressions and decompression (codec) techniques are employed to move digital video from analog to digital and digital to analog formats. Codec trades off the quality of the video for the size of the formats created—the higher the video quality, the larger the memory requirements. This tradeoff becomes significant when you take into account that not only do you need to store video, but you also need to move it around networks in order to be shared and viewed. Compression techniques enable broadcasters to move greater amounts of high-quality video over their cable and satellite networks to viewers.

Many cable television operators convert traditional analog cable television into digital television. Digital television allows cable operators to compress more channels into the digital signal, thus offering integrated-service consumers more choice of programming for the same operating cost of the signal. The move from VHS tape to digital video disks (DVD) is a similar analog-to-digital format conversion. The advantages of moving to a digital DVD format lies in additional entertainment programming and greater navigation options. (Not to mention that one no longer needs to rewind the VHS tape after watching.)

Processing Power

Moore's Law states that processing power doubles roughly every eighteen months. When visual experiences are captured in digital formats, this enhanced processing power can be put to use in new and exciting ways. Consumers can manipulate video and images on their personal computer, achieving affects similar to professional photography retouching at a fraction of the cost. For example, consumers can modify personal digital images and video on personal computers to remove an unwanted scene or eliminate "red eye" in the picture they wish to send to grandma. Advanced processing power also makes it possible to perform more complicated graphic manipulations for video gaming. Rich graphic and complex animation help make virtual worlds seem almost real. Specialized graphics processors are optimized to process images and project them to a screen for viewing. The more powerful the graphic processing capability, the more realistic the image or video can be for the viewer. Game consoles such as Microsoft's Xbox, Nintendo's GameCube, and Sony's PlayStation all possess ever-increasing graphics processing power in order to provide smoother, richer, and more intense gaming experiences.

Digitally Based Networks

Cable television operators were greatly constrained by the amount of bandwidth consumed by analog video. Each channel basically took network bandwidth whether the programming was being watched or not. Digitally based networks offer greater flexibility and bandwidth optimization. Packet-based networks also provide one other important distinction for interactive video services—*a back channel*. A back channel is a means by which the terminal device, such as a cable television set-top box, is able to send digital information back into the network. Traditional broadcast networks send the video signals in one direction, from the broadcaster to the viewer. With truly interactive networks, the viewer can now send information back to the broadcaster or to other viewers. Interactive, packet-based networks make it possible for the gamers to interact with others online or for the viewer to tell the broadcaster which video they would like to watch and when they want to watch it.

Consumer Expectations

Peoples' expectations are shaped by the manner in which they consume visual experiences. The more technology allows consumers to control the timing and sequence of television programming, the more consumers expect to maintain that level of control through digital video recorders and other devices. Digital, networked technologies make it economic for manufacturers to provide consumers with new ways to consume their visual experiences. Each new technology raises consumer expectations for how interactive devices and networks change the visual experience.

Different factors impact consumer expectations of visual imagery technologies, including the following:

◾ Cost—How the consumer views the imagery impacts how the consumer values the service. If someone watches a television broadcast of a movie, the person expects to pay nothing. If that same person rents a movie, he or she expects to pay a modest sum. Finally, if the person buys the movie on DVD, he or she expects to pay more even more. Same movie, different prices, depending on the control exerted over how the movie is run.

The person has no control over when the television broadcast is run (or how commercials are playing during the showing). The person expects to pay a small sum for the convenience of renting the movie for a few days and a larger sum for owning the movie to play on demand. The level of control the viewer exerts helps determine the value placed on the visual imagery.

◼ **Reliability**—When you purchase a product, you expect the product to work as advertised for the period of the warranty (and hopefully well beyond). When you enter into a service relationship, you expect everything to work as advertised as long as you are paying your monthly service fees. The expectations are often greater for the cable television service than the television device itself.

◼ **Availability**—When you wish to rent a video, you know you can only do it during the hours of operation of the video rental store. A pay-per-view (PPV) movie from your cable television or satellite television provider should be available twenty hours a day, seven days a week. As a service, pay-per-view must be always available to the user.

◼ **Selection**—When you enter a physical video or gaming store, a person expects that the inventory on the store shelves is available purchase. A consumer expects much more from a subscription video-on-demand (VOD) service. Since VOD allows providers to digitize and make available any film, consumers expect to choose from a huge virtual inventory.

◼ **Simplicity**—The product or service should "just work." The consumer shouldn't need to understand the technology or spend long periods of time with setup and integration.

The manner in which the consumer experiences visual images shapes the consumer's expectations of the media. The visual experience dictates how the user expects to control the timing, pricing, and management of the visual imagery. The distribution of visual experiences falls into the following five categories: service, retail, rental, broadcast, and performance.

Service

Cable and satellite television provide video as a service. A service model requires a company to act as a network operator. The viewer expects to receive programming from the cable or satellite network provider. This service requires establishing a relationship between the consumer and the network operator. The relationship involves billing (payment for the service) as well as customer service (response to user issues and questions). Consumers generally expect an extremely high level of performance from network operators, since the consumer pays for continuous, reliable access to television content. Consumers view cable and satellite television operators as utilities like electric, water, or phone service. As a result, the expectations from the consumer for twenty-four- hours-a-day, seven- days-a-week operations are high. Cable and satellite operators need to recoup their costs over an extended relationship with the customer. The network providers offset the cost of providing the service with a combination of the following factors: long-term billing relationship (subscriptions), reduction in support costs (Web-based support sites and simplified user instructions), and a willingness to subsidize the consumer's initial need for basic equipment to connect to the network (cable set-top box). By driving down the overhead in maintaining the customer account while encouraging customer loyalty, network operators try to balance the customer requirements for an "always on," rich entertainment service against the service's maintenance cost.

Video Retail

Consumer electronics are primarily sold through a retail model. Unlike the service model, the consumer does not expect to have an extended relationship with the retailer (unless a service agreement is part of the purchase). Consumer electronic devices sold through traditional retail channels can also impact the other distribution models. For example, the sale of personal digital video recorders such as TiVo through retail channels affects the value of broadcasters' advertising, which in turn threatens the ability of television broadcasters to offer high-value content. DVRs enable consumers to record network television shows and skip through the advertising. The devices allow the consumer to watch programming at a time of his or her convenience, without commercials. Such devices can undermine the broadcast television model by reducing the reach of advertisers on the network.

The consumer electronic retail channel can also help other distribution models by encouraging consumer demand for new services. For example, the success of the DVD movie rental model depends on the number of DVD players sold through the traditional retail channels. Since DVDs are a fast-growing market (with purchases up 111 percent between 2000 and 2001), DVD rentals have a rapidly expanding base of potential consumers.[1]

Rental

New technologies like video-on-demand blur the line between the service model and the rental model. In the traditional movie rental business, an operator like Hollywood Video or Blockbuster offers a wide selection of movies for the customer to select, rent for several days, and then return. The penalty fees for late returns can be steep for the consumer and constitute a significant profit for the rental operator.

Pay-per-view and video-on-demand are rental-based business models provided by the cable and satellite television industry as a value-added service beyond the base subscription. These two features are extremely important to the cable and satellite operators from a revenue perspective. These two options help reduce subscriber churn—VOD can reduce churn for digital subscribers by as much as 2 percent. A recent consumer survey found that 63.4 percent of

---

1. Yonish, Steve. "Benchmark May 2002 Data Overview: Covers Digital Decade Forecasts, Device Ownership, Security and Wireless," Boston: Forrester Research, Inc., May 2002.

satellite subscribers purchased pay-per-view programming.[2] As with the video rental model, the consumer selects from a variety of shows and pays a fee to access the entertainment. Since the cable and satellite operator broadcasts the entertainment to multiple households at a single time, however, the service operator can provide the movie at a cheaper price than the movie rental operator. The cable and satellite operators use volume to drive down their costs of transmission and can pass along those savings to the customer. A video store like Blockbuster is able to rent only a single DVD or VHS cassette to a customer, while a service operator provides a single transmission of video to any number of customers. The service operator also offers the consumer the convenience of not going to the video rental store to pick up the movie. These challenges from the service model, driven by the technology that enables PPV and VOD, force the rental operators to explore new ways to attract consumers.

One successful gambit has been the introduction of DVD movies into rental operators' inventory. DVDs provide the consumer with rich content in addition to the movie, such as actor interviews and extra scenes. The DVD inventory gives rental operators the ability to offer consumers content that is not available from the cable and satellite operators. As services expand for cable and satellite operators, the service and rental models will continue to vie for the same consumers, spurred by customer expectations of conveyance, content, and cost for at-home entertainment.

Broadcast

Broadcast television has been around since the inception of the television industry. Advertising during programming supports the broadcast model. The amount of viewers and the demographics of the viewers dictate the value of advertising slots in a given program.

---

2. Yonish, Steve. "Benchmark May 2002 Data Overview: Covers Digital Decade Forecasts, Device Ownership, Security and Wireless," Boston: Forrester Research, Inc., May 2002.

If a television show does not attract enough of the target audience, broadcasters generally pull the show from the programming. The broadcasters completely control the content available on the television network. Consumers have the choice of watching or not watching a program, but have no input into the scheduling or the selection of content. Technologies such as those used in DVRs undermine the broadcast model by providing the consumer with the ability to control the timing and selection of content. A DVR allows the consumer to record television programs for viewing on the consumer's schedule and, if desired, without commercial interruptions. Advertisers do not have the certainty that their ad is going to be watched at the expected time or even at all. For example, an ad slot during the dinner hour costs more for a fast food company but is expected to yield more results than a midafternoon slot. However, if the programming is taped by a DVR, the advertiser has no control over when the ad will be viewed. Despite the premium rate for the ad slot in the programming, the ad itself might be seen at a time when the audience is not thinking about food. Like the retail model, the broadcast model must find ways to add value to the consumer as new technologies raise customer expectations of control in programming.

Performance

In the performance model, the provider offers a set schedule for displaying entertainment. Consumer choice lies in deciding to go to the performance. The consumer is not able to dictate the timing nor the venue of the performance. The consumer selects the preferred showing and pays the provider to access the entertainment. The performance model is least affected by customer expectations since the customer is restricted to a limited role and has no input into the schedule of the showing or even the content of the entertainment. Film studios control the lifetime of a film, from the initial release of a movie through television broadcast.

The consumer has no control over when the film appears as a video rental or on network television. In the performance model,

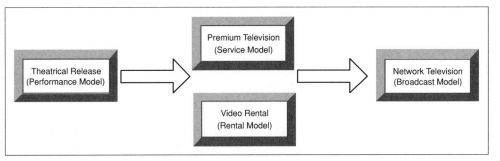

FIGURE 4-1. Consumer's Expectations in Distribution Pipeline

consumer expectations have little impact on the distribution of the visual experience.

Distribution Model

As depicted in Figure 4-1, the distribution model shapes consumer expectations for the visual experience. Consider the movie business as an example. Traditionally, films are first released in movie theaters. The film distributors dictate which theaters show the movie and the movie theater determines the showtimes. The consumer has little control over the viewing experience other than to select a convenient time and place to view the movie. In the performance model, consumer expectations for controlling the viewer experience are dictated by the creators and distributors of the movie.

The next step in the distribution pipeline, video, falls into both the service and rental models. These models provide consumers with a degree of control over the viewing of the movie. Because the consumer has several days to watch the movie, the consumer picks his or her own time and location. The consumer also has the ability to see the movie as part of a cable or satellite provider's VOD or PPV service. Consumers' expectations of service are the lowest in the broadcast model. If the movie is made available on broadcast television, the consumer expects a longer showtime due to television commercials as well as no control over scheduling. At each step in the distribution pipeline, consumer expectations are shaped by the consumer's control (or lack thereof) over the media.

THE DIGITAL DARKROOM

Digital photography changes both the tools of photography as well as the practice of taking pictures. As technologies like digital editing become more accessible, amateur photographers can develop professional production quality video capture and authoring. This heightened degree of control over the visual medium raises consumers' expectations of the devices that capture the imagery, the editing tools, and even the medium for transporting and sharing the images electronically.

Consumer photography has seen the manufacturers of cameras and the providers of film split in strategy. Camera manufacturers, such as Olympus and Nikon, provide filmless (digital) cameras. These devices store images in digital format in physical memory in the camera. Disposable cameras clearly emphasize the value of the film over the camera itself.

The two approaches provide consumers with very different value propositions. The disposable cameras put forward by the film companies provide convenience and situational novelty for the amateur photographer. The film companies gamble that a consumer on vacation is not going to buy an expensive underwater camera for their first snorkeling adventure when a disposable camera will do the trick for much less money. However, for the consumer disposable cameras provide no additional control over the film itself.

The filmless, or digital, camera provides unprecedented manipulation of images for photography hobbyists. Users make value judgments on a per-picture basis, choosing whether to save a photo for print or electronic distribution or to delete the image from the camera memory. The digital format of the image also introduces the ability to enhance and share the image electronically. The digital medium of the images raises the expectations for consumers. Rather than simply send a copy of a photo to a relative, a consumer with a digital camera uses the Internet to distribute the image to multiple recipients or computer software to add affects such as blurring to the image. These expectations, in turn, drive the device manufacturers to integrate more photo enhancement features into the cameras. In addition, the consumer expectation of control creates a market for service providers that provide online tools to modify images and store them in online photo albums. Using these online services, amateur photographers are able to accomplish the following:

- Crop shots
- Brighten images
- Sharpen images
- Remove blemishes and "red eye"

Another area of flexibility available to the digital photographer is the ability to add text, borders, or artwork to an image using programs such as Adobe's Photoshop. Software such as Photoshop can also take an image and use special effects such as ripples, twirls, or embossing.

The ability to alter or enhance images leads to new behaviors. If you have a beautiful image, but there is a person in the shot you would rather not have seen standing next to you, imaging manipulation software can enable you to remove the person from the picture. The digital format enables almost any manipulation of the image—color, content, and sizing. Removing a person from an image is the act of altering ones and zeroes in the digital image. On chemically processed film, this process would require actual physical manipulation of the image—a very difficult and a much more costly process to get the same result.

Traditionally, when an amateur photographer has his or her film developed, the photographer receives standard-size images. The photographer can frame the photos or send them via postal mail to friend and family. Digital images offer consumer more options for distribution. Digital images can be sent via email to relatives and friends. Images can be placed on a Web site and shared with the world as Internet scrapbooks. Alternatively, the consumer can choose to print the image using a color printer or an online service like Shutterfly (www.shutterfly.com). Online services offer additional benefits, such as using digital images on customized calendars and cards.

Digital Video

It is a costly process for the average consumer to develop his or her own film or edit his or her own video. Digital video (DV) cameras capture video and store it in a digital format. Storage costs for digital video hampered earlier versions of digital video cameras. As the cost of memory decreased, device manufacturers were able to develop DV cameras that amateurs could afford.

Even with lower cost memory storage solutions, digital video files are still large in size and require high-speed connections in order to move video from capture devices to editing platforms. The adoption of the high-speed interface technologies such as IEEE 1394, otherwise known as FireWire, has made the transfer of video files from DV cameras to editing platforms a much easier and quicker proposition.

Video Editing

Once digital video is on a personal computer, the editor of the video has many options. First, there is the ability to create special effects. While Hollywood studios have taken special effects to a high art, the average person is now able to insert transition techniques or animation into their videos. Sound provides an additional area of enhanced capability. Software tools allow the amateur video editor to perform advanced sound mixing and insertion into video from the desktop computer. This lets the amateur video editor create music videos or insert sound into video frames. The ease by which consumers can modify video content raises the amateur video editor's expectations about both the device and the resulting video.

Sharing Videos

Digital video can be transferred from editing platforms, such as the personal computer, to a DVD, which can be sent to friends and families. Because of the size of video files, transferring large video files over average-bandwidth networks can be problematic. One answer is to stream the video over networks. Solutions from Microsoft, Real Networks, and Apple computer make it possible to set up streaming video servers to make video available over the Internet.

Digital photography and video capture demonstrate how the capability of a device can change the consumer's expectation of control over the media. The most popular form of visual imagery has seen similar technology advancements impact consumer behavior and interaction with both devices and programming.

The television experience has been evolving for the past fifty years. Television has moved from black and white to color. Cable and satellite television brought premium channels and the twenty-four-hour news cycle. While the new advancements augment *how* people watch television, those same technologies do not change *why* people watch television. People watch television to be informed and entertained. News, sports, entertainment, and weather live at the core of the television experience. New technologies may not change the reason people watch TV but they will impact the mechanics of interacting with the programming and the television as a device.

Cable television has been making significant investments to change their network infrastructure from an analog network to a digital network. Digital cable subscribers increased from 4.0 million households in 1999 to an estimated 15.1 million households in 2001.[3] The reasons cable networks are shifting to digital networks center on profit and competition. First, digital networks enable cable service operators to provide more channels than analog networks in a cost-effective manner. This enables cable television operators to

---

3. Bernoff, Josh. "Cable's On-Demand Salvation" Boston: Forrester Research, Inc., April 2001.

remain competitive with satellite television with respect to content and selection. Second, digital networks enable television operators to provide a wider array of services such as broadband services, digital telephony service, and VOD. A wider range of services increases the average revenue per subscriber. Finally, digital technologies enable cable television operators to augment their integrated services in order to reduce subscribers from leaving the service. A rich set of premium services might increase the lifetime value of the subscriber relationship and reduce subscriber attrition. The following mantra of the network operator focuses on a careful balance of cost and revenue: reduce cost, increase average revenue per subscriber, and reduce the loss of subscribers. Consumer expectations are rising as a result of the shift to digital networks and the introduction of other digital technologies surrounding their television experience. Two such technology shifts are the adoption of DVD and personal digital video recorders.

VHS to DVD

DVD is a totally digital format for imagery that has affected how consumers view movies. Consumers can play an active role in navigating the video. Like an audio cassette, VHS tape requires rewind or fast forward to find a particular scene of interest. DVD, like an audio CD, enables the viewer to quickly pop into different scenes while still not surrendering the ability to fast forward or rewind if desired. Another benefit is that DVDs do not degrade with use, whereas VHS tape does.

Time Shifting

When viewers watch television shows, the television broadcaster dictates the timing and the content of the programming Viewers must watch programming when the television network wants to show it, with the commercials that the television network has attracted and in the time sequence in which the show has been edited. Digital video recorders let consumers watch favorite shows when it is convenient for the consumer, without commercial interruption. In addition, DVRs give the consumer the option to easily back up the digital images to see a scene again. Since the DVR stores images digitally, the DVR can record and save much more content than a traditional VHS cassette. To combat churn and compete against cable, satellite providers distribute DVR functionality as part of the satellite integrated service.

Digital video recorders store the video stream in a digital format. As a result, the user can quickly and easily navigate to other parts of the video stream. You cannot jump instantaneously from one part of a VHS tape to another, but you can in digital memory. A DVR with two receivers can record shows that you are watching as well as shows on other channels that you are not. As a result of storing the show in a digital format and the ability to monitor multiple channels, a DVR is capable of the following:

- Instant replay—You as the viewer can choose to replay any scene or programming at will because the video stream is being stored while you're watching. Simply jump back in the video stream and then pick up where you left off.

- Pause—DVR's enable you to pause live programming because the DVR is storing the video stream.

- Record shows and skip commercials—Most advertising can be differentiated from the normal network programming, and thus skipped, in the video stream being stored in the DVR.

- Record one show while you watch another—DVRs with dual receivers are capable of tuning to and recording from another channel while you may be watching another show.

The flexibility and power provided by the DVR changes viewer behavior by making the viewer an active participant in the programming. The viewer's personal preferences control how the content is viewed. As DVRs become more popular, cable and satellite providers are working toward integrating DVR capabilities into service set-top boxes. The new set-top boxes with DVR capabilities demonstrate how consumer expectations drive changes into interactive devices.

The adoption of DVRs create problems for the broadcast television distribution model. Imagine if the majority of television viewers in North America started using personal digital video recorders for their favorite shows and started time shifting their viewing. It's likely that many of these viewers would opt to have their DVRs skip the advertising. The television networks, which produce and air these shows, may no longer be able to generate the same amount of advertising revenue. Television would become a less attractive advertising medium. Television broadcasters struggle with how to accommodate the changes in consumers' expectations of control over programming.

The Power of Choice

The power of consumer choice in programming is also seen in digital cable services. Digital cable brings new options to consumers for premium video (and helps reduce subscriber attrition, which averaged 6 percent in 2001).[4]

Physical media and outlets have dominated the video rental business. The traditional video rental business has its shortcomings in convenience and selection. Premium video services from cable service operators offer to improve the video rental experience by not requiring the consumer to leave the house and not having a selection limited by shelf space in the rental store.

Pay-per-View

Rather than comparing directly to the video rental experience, the PPV service is more akin to a home theater experience. Just as in a theater, there is a scheduled time you can watch the video. Figure 4-2 describes how pay-per-view movies are delivered to the household.

If the viewer misses the start time, the viewer is out of luck. Then once the video starts, it plays until it is finished. The viewer cannot fast forward, rewind, or pause the performance. These are all options that VHS and DVD viewers have when they rent a video. The final shortcoming when compared to traditional video rental is that you

---

4. Bernoff, Josh. "How Cable TV Can Beat Satellite, April 2002," Boston: Forrester Research, Inc., April 2002.

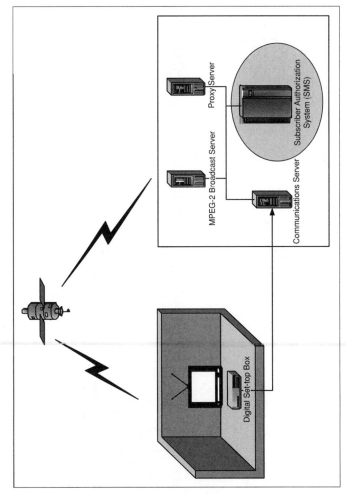

FIGURE 4-2. Pay-Per-View Distribution

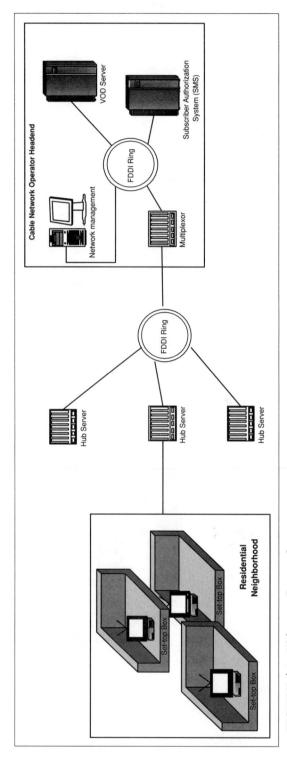

FIGURE 4-3. Video-on-Demand

can see the performance only once rather than as many times as you wish over a particular time period.

Video-on-Demand

Video-on-demand addresses many of the shortcomings of PPV. First, viewers can start the video at their own convenience rather than when scheduled. Second, a designated video stream is sent to the viewer's set-top box. This enables viewers to fast forward, rewind, and pause the video stream.

Depending on the cable operator, the subscriber may even be able to watch the video multiple times during a given time period. VOD is an expensive technology for cable operators to deliver; deployment requires nearly $100 per subscriber.[5] (See Figure 4-3 for an overview of how VOD is delivered to the household.) But even the initial rollouts for VOD (only 3 million of digital cable subscribers had VOD by the end of 2001) are proving highly popular with consumers. One cable operator reports that, of those customers who use VOD, 23% typically buy more than two movies per month. VOD satisfies consumer expectations about choice (providing the ability to pick videos to watch) and schedule (viewing on the consumer's schedule). As a result, VOD subscriptions reduce the amount of digital churn (the percentage of subscribers dropping digital cable service in a given month) from 6 to 4 percent.[6] Cable operators also plan to deploy VOD as a competitive advantage over satellite, which does not support VOD.

Subscription Video-on-Demand (SVOD)

Service providers almost always prefer subscriptionrelationships. Subscription video-on-demand (SVOD) gives viewers the advantages of VOD while having the ability to select from a large catalog of titles. The selection of videos would be highly limited to recently

---

5. Bernoff, Josh. "Cable's On-Demand Salvation," Boston: Forrester Research, Inc., April 2001.
6. Bernoff, Josh. "How Cable TV Can Beat Satellite," Boston: Forrestor Research, Inc., April 2002.

run movies and adult programming. For example, HBO and Showtime offer $3- to $5-a-month subscription VOD (SVOD) services, featuring on-demand access to recent programs. In theory, SVOD offers any show, movie, or sporting event ever produced available to the viewer on request. Cable operators are already seeing strong customer uptake on the model. The SVOD model allows the network operator to set up an ongoing billing relationship with the customer. In return, the consumer obtains access to a wide range of programming. As a result, the SVOD consumer consumes premium programming more frequently then the VOD consumer. One cable operator found that while VOD buy rates exceed one per month for a digital cable subscriber, SVOD usage exceeds seven programs per month.[7]

Interactive TV

The cable and satellite providers also seek to maintain customers through another service: interactive television. Interactive television has gone through many fits and starts over the years. By the end of 2000, only 2.2 million households in the United States had interactive TV (iTV).[8] One of the first issues facing iTV was the very definition of iTV. As a result, iTV has come to mean a number of different capabilities and forms of programming. Rather than debate the merits of one definition or another, we will examine iTV with respect to consumer expectations and show where the iTV movement has exceeded or fallen short of consumer expectations.

At its simplest, iTV is a set of technologies and programming that enable a viewer to provide commands or feedback and affect what they are viewing beyond simple channel selection. At its most ambitious, iTV revolutionizes the viewing experience and augments almost every facet of the viewer's life, from education to shopping.

7. Bernoff, Josh. "How Cable TV Can Beat Satellite," Boston: Forrestor Research, Inc., April 2002.
8. Gluck, Marissa, and Nikki Lewis, Ari Mayerfield, Adrienne Piras, Claudine Singer, Joe Laszlo, Michael May, Seamus McAteer. "Interactive Advertising on Post-PC Platforms: Emphasizing Modal Marketing," New York: Jupitermedia Research, January 22, 2001.

iTV requires a user interface device such as a TV remote or a wireless keyboard for the viewer to provide input. In addition, iTV needs an advanced set-top box connected to the television and the cable connection into the home. Finally, server-side software and hardware need to be running at the cable television provider's head end. The viewer presses commands from his or her keyboard or remote. The set-top box receives the commands. Within the set-top box are a range of applications and middleware that respond to the commands. The application or middleware will interact with the head end to send and retrieve information. The set-top box will then present the information to the television just as a personal computer presents its information to a monitor. While the architecture sounds simple, the challenges are great due to consumer expectations of performance and reliability. The consumer expects any service provided through the television to have the same performance and reliability as the television—a difficult proposition for an emerging technology.

Cable television providers held numerous iTV trials throughout the 1990s. One of the most famous of these trials, which still influences decisions made in the design of iTV integrated services today, was held in Orlando, Florida, in December 1994. Time Warner provided 4,000 homes with advanced services that included video-on-demand, shopping, games, postal service, and an electronic programming guide. The cable provider billed viewers on a pay-per-use model for the services. While the trial was a commercial failure, cable and satellite services learned a key lesson about missed consumer expectations. Subscribers' expectations included the following:

- Cost—The base iTV service should not cost the subscriber anything in addition to their base cable rate. This is highly problematic because the cost of providing iTV integrated services is significant on a per-subscriber basis.

- Simplicity—Many of the people watching the television are not advanced computer users. This means that the user interface must be extremely simple, thus creating a great challenge for the designers of the systems.

▣ Responsiveness—Viewers are used to pressing a button on their remote and getting an instant response whether it's changing the channel or the volume. Latency can exist in iTV systems, as it needs to send information back and forth from the set-top box. Viewers have little tolerance for even a three-second delay.

▣ Applications—Viewers wanted simple and fun applications as part of their iTV service. Gambling and games rank high on the list for desired iTV applications.

There have been numerous advances in iTV since the failure of the Time Warner Orlando trial that have addressed these customer concerns. While still a small market, some analysts predict that 45 million U.S. households will have iTV by 2005.[9] Applications like email and instant messaging are now part of many families' communication patterns. The new iTV applications make both these messaging techniques available through the television. The new model for iTV resolves around *extending* television's role for entertainment while staying within the family-oriented metaphor. An interim step toward truly interactive television is the EPGs. EPG software runs on the set-top box and lets viewers navigate the hundreds of channels that are now available to them. One of the largest providers of EPGs is Gemstar—TV Guide. EPGs provide an interesting case study, as they are an iTV technology that has reached broad adoption.

One of the first reasons EPGs have been successful is their cost structure. EGPs require no significant computing requirements from the set-top box. As a result, EPGs can run on current generation set-top boxes from companies such as Scientific Atlanta and Motorola's General Instruments. This means that the cable service operator does not need to deploy a new set-top box to provide the capability to

9. Gluck, Marissa, and Nikki Lewis, Ari Mayerfield, Adrienne Piras, Claudine Singer, Joe Laszlo, Michael May, Seamus McAteer. "Interactive Advertising on Post-PC Platforms: Emphasizing Modal Marketing," New York: Jupitermedia Research, January 22, 2001.

their subscribers. Second, the EPG is relatively easy to use. The EPG requires only the television remote for the viewer to navigate. Finally, the EPG performs a function that provides a great deal of value to the viewer. It would be extremely difficult to navigate through the hundreds of channels without the assistance of an electronic programming guide. The success of the EPG in training the consumer to use the remote control as a more sophisticated navigation tool paves the way for additional interactive cable and satellite services such as Web-based content, email, and interactive gaming.

THE RISE OF GAMING

Video games in the home have evolved dramatically over the past twenty-five years. Television video gaming has evolved from the early days of "Pong" through more modern systems by Atari and Sega to advanced graphic systems from Sony, Nintendo, and Microsoft. Advances in memory, processing power, and networking have created gaming experiences that raise your pulse and can draw you in for hours of entertainment. What were originally integrated services for hobbyists and technology enthusiasts has grown into an industry that generated over $6.4 billion dollars in revenue in 2001.[10] The video game industry remains an industry moving at an incredible pace.

Game Consoles

Gamer expectations are constantly on the rise. Game consoles are the computing platforms on which the games run. They have user input controls, processing power, and graphics processing power, and many now have networking built into them. The processing horsepower of the platform determines how realistic the game animation will become. While gamers are drawn to more powerful platforms, at the

---

10. Behr, Mary E. "E3 2002 Preview: Video Games to Take Center Stage," PC Magazine, May 20, 2002.

end of the day, if the most compelling games aren't available to run on that gaming console, the gaming console will not be a commercial success. The quality of the games on the gaming platform is closely related to the power of the platform. Without that symbiotic relationship, neither the device manufacturer nor the software provider would be able to provide consumers with a rich experience. Private and public networks add a new service element to the relationship between device and software.

Game consoles and the games that run on them are geared for competition. Traditionally, gamers played against each other while being in the same room, watching the same television screen, and being hooked into the same game console. Network gaming enables players to compete against other players elsewhere in the world.

The basic architecture of networked games is the presence of end devices (personal computers or game consoles) and a gaming server that is available on a shared network such as the Internet. Gamers can establish gaming sessions with the game server and then have others join that session of the game. The games can range from playing card games to large role-playing games. Massive multiuser domains (MUDs) are computing environments that enroll the different players into gaming sessions and keep track of the interactions between the players and the games.

An example of a successful networked game is Sony's "Everquest." Over 700,000 players from around the world subscribe to the game and play each other. Everquest is known as a role-playing game (RPG), because the gamer takes on the persona of a character and interacts with other gamers' personas online.

The demands of online gaming drive both the network providers and the device providers to accommodate consumers' expectations of speed and experience. Advances in technology don't evolve from entertainment alone. As we explore in the next chapter, consumer concerns about home health, safety, and security also dictate how integrated services evolve.

Monitoring through Devices

5

As interactive services permeate the home, many of the more basic household services such as home security follow the trend toward more sophisticated owner and device interaction. Household devices like alarm systems evolve from stand-alone warning appliances to being networked into frontline sensing devices for interactive services. These networked devices provide owners with the ability to monitor homes remotely. The latest advances in monitoring feature manufacturers networking household sensing devices and tying them into a service center. Monitoring solutions increase safety and security and are evolving into platforms for enhanced productivity. As people have come to adopt and rely on these systems, the reliability and predictability of such systems become increasingly important. Interactive monitoring systems for the home require a high level of reliability because owners will not tolerate downtime from a device as important as a security system.

This chapter explores three ways that interactive technologies are being deployed as monitoring solutions. These advanced monitoring solutions combine the power of location-determining technologies, sensors, and networked service centers. First, we explore how telematics make the automobile safer and easier to maintain. Second, we describe personal safety solutions ranging from personal emergency response systems to embedded monitoring health systems. And finally, we examine how the home is becoming safer through networked security systems.

After reading this chapter, you should have a good understanding of the following topics:

■ What enabling technologies are powering interactive monitoring systems

■ How consumers are using these new monitoring systems to be safer, healthier, and more productive

■ How telematics, embedded health monitoring systems, and home security systems have moved alarm systems into the realm of interactive services

INTERACTIVE MONITORING

Home security, health, and family well-being are high priorities to most people. Unexpected circumstances need to be identified so corrective action can take place. With advances in sensor technology and communication networks, monitoring solutions are becoming more pervasive in American homes and automobiles.

These interactive systems are composed of sensing devices, a local control and communications unit, and a service center. The sensing devices are special-purpose sensors that collect information about their environment. Their environment could be a room in a house, the engine of a car, or a pumping heart. The sensor sends the collected information to a local control-and-communications unit. This unit collects information from a number of sensors and determines if any the information constitutes the triggering of some action. In some cases, a local indication provides a visual or audio alert to indicate that action needs to take place. This feedback could be as simple as a light going off on the dashboard of your car or an in-home fire alarm sounding off. The communications part of the control unit then notifies a service center that something requiring attention has taken place. Service center responses range from notifying a medical professional that his or her attention is required to deploying road-side assistance or sending local law enforcement to check out a home. While the initial deployment of such systems and services focuses on safety and security, it is possible that a service center will be able to provide richer and richer value-added services over time. We explore some of the value-added services when we examine automotive telematics.

Interactive monitoring services have been deployed for military and commercial use for many years. More recently, cost-effective electronics, software, and telecommunications have made such systems more affordable to the consumer. Interactive monitoring services exist at the nexus of location technology, sensor technology, and communication technology.

Enabling Technologies

As mentioned earlier, monitoring solutions have made an evolutionary leap from stand-alone alarm systems to integrated safety and security solutions. The cost-effective development of enabling technologies is at the heart of making such systems available to the general public. In previous chapters, we discussed the advances in wireless and data communications. Two other significant technologies that fuel the adoption of interactive monitoring solutions, location technologies, and sensor technologies remain.

Location Technologies

If a person's security is to be monitored, then the ability to monitor that security needs to travel with the person. When someone needs assistance, those who are coming to the rescue need to know where the person in need is located. Location technology provides position information so that assistance personnel can quickly locate the person in need. The two location technologies we cover are global positioning systems (GPS) and enhanced 911 (E911) wireless technology.

Global Positioning System

One of the greatest navigational challenges in the history of the world has been determining one's location at any given point in time. Two coordinates, latitude and longitude, help identify every location on the face of the Earth. Calculating latitude and longitude was a critical function of ship navigators and remains so to this day. Rather than using a sextant, today's navigators use a different tool: the global positioning system.

During the 1960s, the U.S. military developed a number of systems to augment navigation. In 1973, the U.S. Department of Defense required coordinated efforts on behalf of the different branches of the military to solve the problem. Satellite-based systems continued to evolve until 1978, when the first launches of GPS satellites were launched. In 1983, the U.S. government made the GPS system publicly available to the world. A second set of satellites began to be launched in 1989 that established today's system of satellites.

The GPS consists of a series of at least twenty-four satellites orbiting the Earth that send out timed signals measured to the precision of atomic clocks. GPS receivers on the Earth determine a specific position by receiving these signals from at least four satellites and making calculations in the time difference between the signals. When a receiver has four such signals, it can then calculate a location in three-dimensional space.

The accuracy of the location depends on the type of receiver and the accuracy of the timing of satellite signals. Before May 2000, timing errors were purposefully inserted into the GPS signals to limit accuracy to 100 meters due to military concerns. Today GPS receivers are able to provide accuracy to within 10 to 20 meters. There are techniques that can be employed that can bring this accuracy to within 1 meter.

GPS systems are used in a number of applications today. These applications include, but are not limited to, use by the military, by ships at sea, and by trucking fleets. More recently, GSP technology has come down in price so that it can be embedded in more everyday devices such as handheld GPS receivers, automobiles, and recreational watercraft. By embedding this technology in cars, it is possible to locate a car after a car accident or even after it has been stolen.

Enhanced 911

Using a similar signal time difference techniques as the GPS system, it is also possible to locate mobile phones by identifying a phone relative to different cellular towers. Today, when someone calls the emergency support number from a landline in the United States, a 911 operator is able to see the address from which the phone call is being made. Think of this as a more complete version of caller ID. As a result of having the address of the caller, emergency personnel can be dispatched to the location of the person in need, even when that person is unable to communicate where they are located. Since wireless phones are mobile, the billing address of the owner does not indicate to a 911 operator where the person is located. This creates a significant dilemma if the person in need cannot communicate their location. As a result, in 1999 the U.S. Federal Communications Commission (FCC) mandated that wireless carriers must adopt location technologies so 911 operators can locate people making emergency phone calls.

The wireless location systems work in the opposite direction from the GPS system. In the GPS system, the *receiver* is trying to determine the position. In the wireless locations systems, the *network* is trying to determine a phone's location. The most common technique is to locate the phone receiving a common signal from the phone at three different cell towers. Every phone identifies itself to the network by sending out a signal. Multiple cell towers receive the signal and determine which tower will provide the best communication service to the phone. In the case of location technology, the multiple towers (in this case three) receive the phone's signal. The towers receive the signals at different times because they are located at different distances from the phone. By calculating the time difference between when the three towers receive the signal, they can determine a location in two dimensions, in the plane that the three towers reside upon (it takes three points to make a plane).

The U.S. FCC requires a certain degree of accuracy for these wireless location technologies. In Phase II of the FCC requirements, a mobile 911 caller's location must be determined within 100 meters 67 percent of the time, and within 300 meters 95 percent of the time.[1] You will note that this degree of accuracy is significantly less than that of the GPS system. While the technology should be capable of greater accuracy, existing requirements have been established in order for it to be practical for wireless carriers to implement the existing technology.

Beyond 911, location-based technology in wireless communications has many commercial applications. Such applications will range from public safety to getting directions to marketing and promotion. These systems also raise significant issues surrounding privacy and law enforcement. While this technology is in its infancy, the potential impact of this technology on daily lives is very significant.

Sensors

Interactive monitoring systems need eyes and ears in order to tell control and communication units what is going on around them. Great advances have been made in the area of sensors. As recently as twenty years ago, the only sensors in an automobile were a tachometer, a battery gauge, a speedometer, and a temperature gauge. Today, there are hundreds of sensors that range from proximity sensors for when a bumper gets too close to an object to sudden motion detectors that tell an airbag to deploy in a fraction of a second.

Advances in sensor technology have made these sensors smaller, more durable to harsh environments, and more accurate in the information that it is gathering about their environment. Sensors cover

1. FCC Wireless 911 Requirements, Federal Communications Commission, January 2001.

a wide range of capabilities and can be grouped in the following categories:

- Pressure sensors
- Temperature sensors
- Motion detectors
- Light detectors
- Quantity meters (gas, water, battery level, etc.)
- Sound detectors
- Chemical detectors
- Radiation detectors

Sensors are designed for specific purposes. Sensors detect variances in light, pressure, sound, the presence of smoke, or other chemical agents. Sensors are designed for a specific level of sensitivity. When that sensitivity is exceeded, the notification mechanism kicks into action.

The interactive monitoring systems are only as reliable and useful as the quality of sensors and detectors that provide frontline information. The ramifications for sensors not providing accurate information can be devastating. As people continue to incorporate more and more interactive monitoring systems into the daily lives, they are becoming increasingly dependent on such systems. Many complex systems, such as an automobile, use these sensors to aide in self-diagnosis.

Automotive Telematics

The modern automobile has evolved into a highly interactive computing device coupled to the internal combustion engine. Traditionally, sensors in a car functioned like an alarm system. If the gas gauge went below an acceptable level, a light would go on telling the driver that he or she should get some gas. Telematics combine computing and communication technologies. Automotive telematics combine sensors in a car with wireless communications and location technologies. Through telematics, automobiles have become interactive devices that make their drivers safer and more productive. When the sensors are combined with a local command and communication system onboard and a service center at the other end of the communication network, you have a modern interactive monitoring service. One of the best examples of automotive telematics provided in the form of an interactive service is the OnStar system. General Motors first conceived what was to become the OnStar system in 1995. By 1997, the OnStar system was deployed in the Cadillac. In 2002, GM had over 2 million subscribers to the OnStar service and has begun to move the interactive service into other automobile lines in the GM family.[2]

The primary value proposition of the OnStar system is to provide an integrated communications system to enhance driver safety and security. The services range from airbag deployment notification to roadside assistance to remote diagnostics about the car's health. The system has evolved significantly in a short period of time, tackling significant issues around user interface, location, and communications.

The user interface of the OnStar system is primarily provided through verbal communication. Having a visually rich interface would take the driver's eyes off the driving environment. Drivers can more safely talk and drive at the same time as long as their hands can remain on the steering wheel and not try to hold a phone at the same time. Cars that have the OnStar system have an integrated system that consists of sensors throughout the car, a GPS receiver, and wireless communications. In the event that the car is stolen or an accident has happened, the OnStar system can quickly determine the location of the car anywhere through the GPS system and then provide that information back to the OnStar service center. The

2. General Motors OnStar corporate Web site, July 15, 2002.

sensors in the car can determine if an airbag has been deployed or if the engine is not functioning within acceptable parameters. When drivers lock themselves out of their automobiles, they can call the OnStar service center and have the doors unlocked remotely.

But the safety and security aspects of such systems are only the beginning. While safety and security is the initial motivator for the consumer to adopt such systems, the consumer can learn about other capabilities of the system and learn new behaviors. Automotive telematics provide a platform on which more interactive services can be deployed for productivity and entertainment. For example, in order to make drivers more effective, such systems can provide direction assistance based on the location of the car, the address of the destination, and the mapped road information between the two points. When running low on gas, such services can inform you of the closest and potentially cheapest gas station relative to your current location. And finally, personal concierge services can be employed to locate and book the best hotels and attractions while you are on a road trip.

PERSONAL HEALTH MONITORING

Connecting the wide array of personal test equipment to interactive networks is the next step in converting stand-alone test equipment into cost-effective preventive care monitoring. Aging increases health-related issues and drives up treatment costs. Health organization demand more cost-effective approaches to health services. Elderly people seeking home-based health solutions have been growing dramatically in the United States. The National Association for Home Care estimates that there were over 20,000 providers of home health care services to 7.6 million people in 2001.[3] Personal health

---

3. Health Care Financing Administration, Office of the Actuary, March 2001.

monitoring is being promulgated as one approach to increase the quality of life while bringing costs into alignment with the ability to pay.

Personal health monitoring is the use of sensors to relay information to the patient or the doctor about the status of a health condition. A wide array of sensor and home testing technology has been developed to provide more extensive monitoring of a health condition while not requiring a patient's visit to a busy clinic. Personal health monitoring technology can be applied to blood pressure, heart rate, and blood sugar levels or even be used as an emergency notification device. This same technology can also be used to help locate and call for emergency medical assistance.

Preventative Care Monitoring

Aging patients have many conditions that can be monitored from the comfort of their home. Personal testing equipment for blood pressure, heart rate, cholesterol, and blood sugar are available at the local drug store. The first applications for preventive care monitoring are being explored in postoperation release of patients from the hospital. The patient rents, leases, or buys monitoring equipment that is specially configured to communicate with the medical institution. As the patient periodically takes tests from home, the data from these tests are sent to the medical institution for analysis. This dramatically reduces the amount of time the patient needs to spend in the hospital and leaves hospital bed space to the most critical needs of patients requiring round-the-clock personal observation.

Digital Angel demonstrates how one manufacturer combines the capabilities of health sensors, location technologies, and wireless communications. The company provides devices with sensors that can monitor heart rate or blood sugar levels and provide that information over digital wireless communications networks. The devices can take many forms, from a bracelet to a handheld device to a device resembling a pager.

One class of patients who are of particular interest for health and location monitoring are Alzheimer patients. By wearing a device, a lost Alzheimer's patient could be identified. In addition, the device can provide special medical information such as what drugs are currently prescribed to the patient and known allergies. The medical information can be easily downloaded to hospital personnel at the hospital or at the scene of a medical emergency.

Personal Emergency Response Systems

The challenge of the elderly finding themselves alone and in a medical emergency is a very real situation. Personal Emergency Response Systems (PERS) are an interactive service that enables a person in need to quickly contact someone and receive assistance.

A PERS is comprised of three major components:

◧ Transmitter

◧ Communications console

◧ Emergency response center that monitors requests

The combination of these elements creates an interactive, networked safety service for those in need.

Transmitters are typically small devices that can be carried by the person in the form of a necklace or bracelet. Sometimes these transmitters attach to a belt or are placed in a pocket. The transmitter has a single button that can be pressed when a person is in need. When the button is pushed, the transmitter sends a radio signal to the communication console.

When the communications console receives a signal from the transmitter, the console moves into action. Typically, the communications console is connected to the phone service and places a call to an emergency response center. The communications console notifies the emergency response center of the identity of the caller and then typically switches to a speakerphone mode.

An employee at the emergency response center receives the call from the communication console with the following information:

telephone number, address, medical history, allergies, hospital preference, a list of contact persons, and the primary physician's name and phone number. The employee at the emergency response center tries to talk with the person in need over the communication console's speakerphone to determine the nature of the situation. The employee then calls the appropriate contacts in order to assist the person in need.

SECURITY MONITORING

Home alarm systems have been in existence since before the turn of the century. The home generally contains a person's greatest amount of personal property. Protecting that personal property and your family becomes an important task. Interactive security integrated services that combine sensors, telecommunications, and service centers elevate home security solutions to a level well beyond door locks and fire detectors.

Traditionally, locks exist on doors and windows to keep unwanted people from gaining access to your home. With traditional alarm systems, if anyone were home, they would be notified that there had been a breach of security. The person would then have to respond to the alarm by investigating the breach or calling public services. Networking a home security system into service centers creates a new class of security services. The home can now be monitored and action taken when no one is home. The response of local law enforcement and fire personnel can be much more rapid when notified by the service center.

How Home Monitoring Works

Home monitoring is an interactive system with many components.

■ Sensors—Sensors detect variances in light, movement, and other factors in the environment.

■ Control Console—The control console or panel provides the homeowner a central place where they can activate, deactivate, and change settings for the monitoring. The control console also communicates with the monitoring center when needed.

■ Monitoring Center—Through communication networks, the control console sends a message to a centralized monitoring center run by a home monitoring company (see Figure 5-1). The home monitoring company has information concerning the home, including address, phone numbers, and past history. Personnel at the monitoring center will try to determine if it is a false alarm or not by calling the home. If they cannot confirm that it is a false alarm, then they will contact local public safety to have the incident investigated.

A home alarm system sets off a signal when undesired circumstances trigger a sensor. Such undesired circumstances include a door being opened in the middle of the night, a window broken, or even motion in the home when everyone should be in their bed. Traditionally, when such triggers went off, the alarm system would use simple logic to determine whether it might be a false positive from a sensor. In the event that the alarm system thought it was a true signal from the sensor, the system would leap into action and sound a loud noise and possibly lights.

Another notification system within the home is the fire alarm system. Fire alarms have been instrumental in saving many lives over the years. These alarm systems have sensors that are constantly on the lookout for fire in the home. When smoke reaches a detector and is above a particular strength level, the alarm is triggered. The alarm sends out a loud sound signal to notify everyone in the home it has detected something potentially dangerous. The alarm needs to be loud enough to wake people from deep sleep.

In the case of intruders or fire, homeowners desire not only to be notified quickly of impending danger but also to put public safety

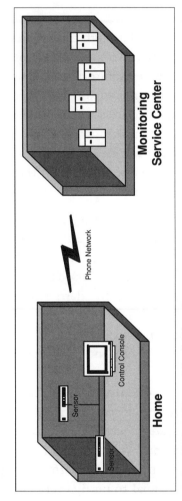

FIGURE 5-1. Home Monitoring System

systems into effect as quickly as possible. To give homeowners a greater sense of control and notify local public safety authorities, these home security and fire alarm systems can now be hooked into a monitoring network with a home monitoring company such as ADT or Brinks Home Security.

When an alarm is triggered, if there is anyone in the home at the time, the alarm will alert him or her to danger. In the event that no one is home, or the people at home are unable to respond to the pending danger, the home monitoring company receives notification. From the point of receiving notification, the home monitoring company attempts to determine the circumstances of the situation. The home monitoring company calls the home to see if it is a false alarm. In the event that the home monitoring company cannot confirm that it is a false alarm, the home monitoring company notifies the appropriate authorities to investigate the situation. This results in more timely involvement by fire, rescue, or police departments.

Family Monitoring

Interactive services for monitoring extend to the members of the family as well as the house itself. New devices that enable parents to keep track of their children have been entering the marketplace. These technologies range from Web cams to GPS-enabled bracelets to data-capable mobile phones. With an increasingly mobile society, more knowledge about risks to our children, and busier schedules, parents are seeking tools that enable them to monitor the well-being of their children. These new devices range in interactivity from the low end of audio-based baby monitors, to the high end of daycare Web cameras and GPS locating bracelets.

In the Cradle

An effective education campaign has led to greater and greater knowledge surrounding sudden infant death syndrome (SIDS). The cause of SIDS is unknown but many doctors suspect that the condition is related to the position of the baby when sleeping. In order to monitor the well-being of a sleeping baby, radio-controlled baby monitors have been in the market for a number of years and are often seen at a baby shower.

Baby monitors typically consist of a two-component system, the transmitter and the receiver. The transmitter is placed wherever the baby is sleeping. The transmitter has a microphone in it and transmits sounds from the room over a radio signal. The receiver stays with the parent, takes in the radio signal from the transmitter, and plays it at a volume set by the parent. The radio signal is limited in range to prevent interference with monitors in other homes. This technology is a natural extension of "walkie-talkies" that many children have played with over the years.

Baby monitors are becoming more and more advanced. The newest wave of baby monitors send a video signal to the receiver in order to provide a visual image of the baby as well as the accompanying audio of the baby's environment.

Daycare Monitoring

Many daycares now provide parents with the ability to view their children over a streamed video feed from a camera in the daycare to their computers at work over the Internet. The ability to view your children in daycare over the Internet has affectionately become known as "nanny cams."

Nanny cams consist of the following components: a PC camera, personal computers, the Internet, and streamed video player on the parent's computer. A wireless or serial PC camera is connected to a computer at the daycare center. This computer acts as a server providing both a Web site and the streamed video feed from the camera. The daycare computer is connected to the Internet through an Internet service provider. The parents at work have access to the Internet through their business connection. The parent visits the daycare Web site, selects the streamed video feed, and views what's going on that day in daycare. To view the image, the parent requires a player that can handle the format of the streamed video. Such players include Microsoft's Media Player, Real Networks' RealOne Player, or Apple's QuickTime.

Security

Interactive monitoring services introduce new challenges along with their many obvious benefits. As it becomes easier for people to use technology to monitor their homes and members of the household, concern about security and privacy increases along with device usage. Most of these issues around monitoring are nontechnical in nature, such as privacy, but potentially require technical solutions.

Interactive monitoring solutions can carry very personal information. Many of these systems can also send commands to the devices with which they interact. Because of the networked component of all of these systems, a breach of network access could create a significant breach of security. For example, automotive telematic systems make it possible to unlock car doors. It would also be possible to turn off home security systems for illegal entry. Technology that creates security also introduces the means for breaching those same barriers. There are two components of security that could create the most logical point of entry for someone desiring to do harm.

The first point of entry is the communications network. Encryption technology can be employed to provide greater amounts of security around data communications between the control units and the service centers. Today's reality is that encryption technology is not universally utilized and even when it is, the strength of the encryption used is often not considered "strong" encryption. As time progresses and the types of monitored data become more sensitive, stronger forms of protection will need to be deployed to secure the data communications network.

The second point of entry is the service center, due to the "human factor"—that is, the response system managed by personnel. Prevention of unscrupulous employees misusing information and access to peoples' security systems requires additional security measures within the service center's infrastructure. The service provider's systems need to contain role-based authorization for actions by their personnel. Role-based authorization restricts personnel to prescribed actions that fall within a given position. For example, the service center software can have two roles, one as Administrator and the other as Dispatch. Personnel whose job it is to call the household when an alarm has been triggered are assigned to the Dispatch role while managers might be assigned to Administrator. The service center software then restricts access to information in the system to only what the particular role requires for their action. Personnel assigned to the Dispatch role might only see the household's phone number and the triggered alarm's identification. Those assigned to the Administrator role could see all the information about the homeowner, including billing method and history.

The service center's system also requires strong audit and logging capabilities. If a security breach does occur within the service center, logs that track who has access to what information and which actions are taken help investigators determine the source of the breach.

PRIVACY

Interactive monitoring systems contain a great amount of information about your identity, health, and behaviors. The consumer needs to trust that the service provider will not misuse information. Today, that trust does not exist. When asked by Forrestor Research, 82 percent of respondents did not believe a company's claim that they would not sell their personal data to other companies.[4] Personal information around identity, health, and behaviors has great value to marketers and is often sold and resold. The challenge surrounding

---

4. Kolko, Jed. "Who Consumers Trust With Personal Data," Boston: Forrester Research, June 7, 2002.

what is private and what is public will rage for years to come. To give consumers control over their personal information, many service providers allow customers to dictate how their personal information is shared. Customers can either call service centers or use Web sites that let them set parameters on how they are contacted for marketing offers or how their information is shared with other companies. As with any technological advancement, with the advantages come risks. The flow of information across radio and telephone lines provides safety and security for homeowner while introducing complex issues of what constitutes privacy in a networked world. As devices and their interactive services become more commonplace in the home, these questions will become more important to consumers.

6 Balancing Act

As devices become more common in the household, interactive services have evolved from a novelty into a common occurrence in people's lives. In order for integrated services to develop into a daily necessity, consumers need confidence that the technology and services are truly reliable. Integrated services provide the promise of a ubiquitous network with access to an array of information and media-rich services through increasingly powerful devices. Delivering on the promise involves significant challenges. The adoption of new devices and the resulting changes of consumer behavior create new expectations. Consumers expect reliability and ubiquitous access to service. Consumers also demand that services and devices will continue to improve with minimal inconvenience to the consumer when upgrading. This chapter explores the balancing act between increased consumer adoption and the requirements placed upon the providers of integrated services to meet such demands.

After reading this chapter, you should have a good understanding of the following topics:

- ▣ The role of infrastructure for integrated services

- ▣ Which enabling technologies contribute to next generation infrastructures

- ▣ How continued consumer adoption affects learned behavior surrounding ubiquitous access, dependence, and continuous upgrading of services

FROM NOVELTY TO NECESSITY

As people continue to incorporate integrated services into their lives, consumers begin to rely on the information and services to a greater extent. This shift from novelty to necessity places substantial requirements upon the providers of integrated services. The concept of reliance on a service is not new. Power utilities, telecommunication utilities, and financial institutions have lived with such requirements for over a hundred years. These are large entities that have deployed infrastructures based on physical or analog processes to provide an array of critical services to consumers. Today, the new infrastructures are based on computing technologies, digital formats, and digital communication networks. These new infrastructures have evolved on top of traditional infrastructures. In some cases, the new technologies have either entirely or partially replaced the older services. Consider how automated telling machines have reduced the reliance on human interaction at the bank branch or how Web-based stock trading facilities for financial institutions have supplemented phone-based trading and visits to the broker's office. Sometimes the technology improvements are significant enough to warrant a shift in the entire infrastructure of the network.

Any of these companies will tell you that providing an infrastructural service to consumers is not an easy task. Significant requirements exist. First, there is the notion of ubiquitous access. When consumers view a service as a necessity rather than a convenience, the provider of the service need to make it universally accessible. Electricity, telecommunication services, and banking services have been built out to reach urban and rural communities alike. Along with ubiquitous access comes the requirement of access anytime. Consumers expect their electricity to be on twenty-four hours a day, seven days a week. The same is true of their phone service or an automated teller machine. The final aspect of utility service expectation is reliability. Service outages must be few and far between, and when outages do occur, the system is expected to "fail gracefully." This means that no harm is done to consumers, their devices, or other assets when the system fails and eventually comes back online.

Providing a service infrastructure that can meet such reach and reliability requirements is a daunting and expensive endeavor. Cable television providers and wireless carriers have spent billions of dollars building out their digital network infrastructures. As the next generation of service infrastructure surrounding information and media assets continues to evolve from novelty to necessity, companies that build out these digital, networked infrastructures continue to be placing expensive bets. These new infrastructures are relying on a new breed of enabling technologies to meet the expectations of consumers. The final challenge in providing a broad-based, essential services infrastructure is interoperability. Interoperability enables different devices and software applications to operate on various underlying platforms by adhering to agreed-upon standards. For example, you can plug any appliance into a power receptacle in the United States because all the manufacturers use the same standards for electrical power outlets. Travel to another part of the world and you will find that the plug may not fit into the power receptacle because a different standard is used in that country. One example of interoperability in the digital integrated services is between computing hardware and software. There are multiple layers (see Figure 6-1) that require interoperability in order for the consumer to receive the benefit of the integrated service. For computing hardware and software, file formats need to be read by applications. Applications need to run on operating systems, and operating systems run on top of devices like personal computers. If any tier is not interoperable with its adjoining tier, then customers will not be able to use the integrated service.

Enabling Technologies

The infrastructures that support today's electrical, telecommunication, and financial services are major modern achievements. These established networks' technologies focus on moving analog or physical

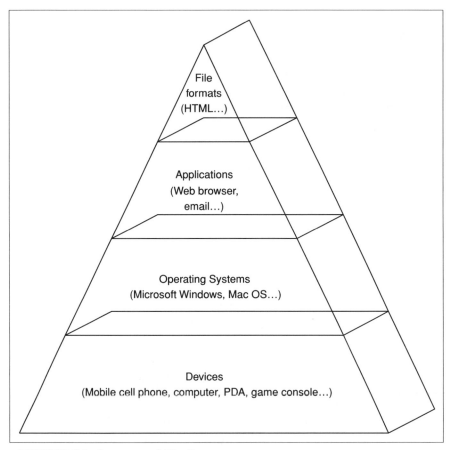

FIGURE 6-1. Interoperability Layers

assets from one point to another. Even when the traditional networks move digital assets (such in an electronic funds transfer), the processes do not transfer well to the emerging world of integrated services. The primary difference between these traditional infrastructures and the emerging interactive service infrastructures are as follows:

🔲 Exclusive focus on managing and moving digitally formatted assets

◫ Real-time system performance requirements

◫ Interoperability with a wide array of devices

Very complex systems are being deployed to manage and distribute digital assets. The more complex a system, the more opportunity exists for quality and compatibility issues. The establishment of common interfaces between devices, networks, and systems mitigates this complexity. The need for a common set of ways to exchange and protect digital assets has moved from a nicety to a necessity.

Standards

Standards exist so that consumers and manufacturers share a common baseline of expectations surrounding quality, interoperability, and safety. Governments mandate some standards while other standards evolve as common commercial practices. Standards have always existed as part of infrastructure technologies. For example, in most countries the voltage at which electricity is provided is standardized so that appliance manufacturers know what to expect in product development. Standards are either established in a standards body or through the commercial adoption of a particular vendors approach. One of the world's most significant standards bodies is the International Organization for Standards (ISO). ISO has representation from 143 national standards bodies and has established more than 13,000 standards for business and governments ranging from the standard format for banking smart cards to the standard speeds for camera film to the standard framework for quality management (ISO 9000).[1] For Internet technologies, an example of a standards body is the Internet Engineering Task Force (IETF). The IETF is an organization of companies, government, and educational institutions that come together and publish standards surrounding the Internet. Standard bodies such as the IETF form working groups that allow

1. ISO in Figures, International Organization of Standards, January 2002.

interested participants to draft new standards and have other members of the working group reply with the thoughts, concerns, and issues. One such standard from the IETF is the next generation of the Internet Protocol (IP). The IP contains addressing and control information that allows packets to be routed around the Internet.

But standards aren't always at the cutting edge of technology. For example, the current standard for the hypertext markup language (HTML) does not take into account special augmentations that have been made by different Web browser companies. Sometimes there is a need for a new capability that the existing standard does not address. When this occurs in a competitive marketplace, companies "embrace and extend" the existing standards. The developers of technology will use an existing standard, but then create an extension to the standard in order to meet the new specific need. When this happens, developers risk building an extension that may not be compatible with how the standard evolves in the future. This leads to potential incompatibilities for companies and their customers. Companies that extend standards hope that their new way of doing things will become a new commercial standard. When a company owns a commercial standard, the financial and technology investment rewards can be significant.

Standards help the designers of different systems interact with other systems like building blocks. The notion of building blocks is important. The range of possible applications running on top of an infrastructure can be so great that the inability for different components to talk with one another jeopardizes the overall quality of the experience for the consumer.

Web Services

As interactive information services move from novelty to necessity, it becomes critical for different systems to be able to exchange information in a standard manner. For example, your medical history may be stored securely in your doctor's computer records and needs to be shared for emergency purposes with a different hospital system. It is important that the hospital computer system be able to read and understand the health record sent from your doctors system. The same will need to be true for a wide array of information ranging from financial services to entertainment. For the new infrastructures, information travels over a common networking protocol called transmission control protocol/Internet protocol (TCP/IP). TCP/IP is the networking protocol used over the Internet. These information services have been grouped under the broad term of "Web services," but should not be mistaken for the information services that are only available via personal computers and the World Wide Web. These Web services will be accessible from mobile phones, interactive television, and personal digital assistants.

Typically, information technology (IT) organizations inside corporations and institutions manage the systems that enable the exchange of information via software applications. These information systems can be highly proprietary systems with a centralized server and customized client applications (client–server architectures). Getting one proprietary client–server system to exchange information with another proprietary client–server system takes considerable work. Often, the interfaces through which these proprietary systems exchange information are incompatible. Web services constitute a dramatically more distributed and open way in which different systems can exchange information. The current standard being worked on by such companies as Microsoft and IBM is called the Web Services Distribution Language (WSDL).

The WSDL is a standard format written in the extensible markup language (XML) that describes how *messages* and *operations* can be exchanged between different services. You can think of the messages as the data that is being exchanged and the operations as the actions that are to be performed. XML is a document format that enables data formats to be defined and exchanged in a much more loosely coupled way than traditional, rigid information systems. WSDL defines the way systems exchange data and request actions of other systems. The manner in which the data exchange occurs between information systems is similar to how current standards enable banks to exchange funds. Such standards are important because they become the foundation upon which consumers and service providers build quality, reliability, and security for infrastructure services.

Grid Computing

The evolution of interactive services requires significant changes in computing architectures. Interactive services require extensive computing resources that are accessible independent of location, time, or the nature of the application being used. Grid computing lies at the heart of infrastructure environments that handle shifting computer processing demands in a cost-effective manner. Just as electric utilities distribute electricity through "grids," grid computing creates a distributed network of computing resources (e.g., processors and memory) for the purpose of tackling a multitude of diverse, computationally intensive applications. The advantage to grids lies in their ability to access underutilized resources in the network and provide higher reliability. In addition, grids offer effective disaster recovery in the event that some portion of the grid becomes unavailable. The notion of distributed computing lies at the heart of grid computing (see Figure 6-2).

Distributed computing is the ability to send processing tasks to multiple computers rather than performing the task on a centralized computer. An example of distributed computing at work is the processing of data from the Search for Extraterrestrial Intelligence at Home (SETI@Home) project. SETI@Home faced a daunting challenge: processing the huge amount of data from scanning the skies for electromagnetic signals coming from space. The amount of computing resources required to perform this task fell beyond normal budgetary constraints for purchasing hardware and software. To solve the problem, SETI@Home created a screensaver that enabled anyone on the Internet to download and process the data. As a result of this distributed computing model, a worldwide network of over 3.8 million computers donated over 1 million years of collective central processing unit (CPU) time to the task.[2]

---

2. SETI@Home Web site (http://setiathome.ssl.berkeley.edu/), July 15, 2002.

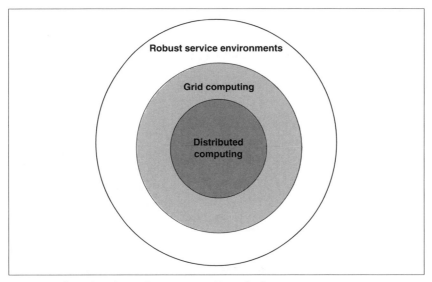

FIGURE 6-2. Service Infrastructure Foundation

By distributing computing resources through a grid of available computers, underutilized computing resources from around the world can be tapped when the demand is needed. When some parts of the computing network are unavailable, other parts of the network can pick up the extra load. Backing up information to multiple locations within a network also simplifies disaster recover from a catastrophic failure. Companies such as IBM, Sun, and Microsoft are working to make this new computing architecture applicable for commercial use. Current projects range from using distributed computing resources for helping to solve cancer to becoming environments for massive multiuser domains for interactive gamers.

Security Technologies

Making interactive services mainstream also requires dealing with more and more sensitive data. Legal, health, and financial information need to be securely stored and transferred between systems. Administrators need to protect systems against malicious attack to ensure that service does not fail at a critical moment. The number of reported security-related incidents has grown dramatically over the past decade. The CERT Coordination Center at Carnegie Mellon University's Software Engineering Institute has been charged with tracking security incidents by the U.S. Defense Advanced Research Projects Agency. Since 1990, such reported incidents have grown from 252 to over 52,000 in 2001.[3] The topic of security technology is a varied and complex subject too great to cover in detail in this section. However, a flavor for some of the mainstream technologies that are being deployed to meet basic security needs can be explored here. Two such technologies are the Secure Socket Layer (SSL) protocol and firewalls.

Secure Socket Layer

Interactive services involve the transfer of digital information across communication networks. As data are traveling across data networks, a number of undesirable actions can take place. Data can be altered (such as a student changing his or her grades), communications can be eavesdropped on (people reading your email or chat communications), or someone can try to impersonate you (steal your credit card number and use it for illegal purchases). The Secure Socket Layer (SSL) is a security technology that helps to thwart such activity for Web-based interactions.

SSL allows two parties to disguise the information that they are passing to one another over the WorldWide Web by encrypting (scrambling) the information, transferring the data to another party, and then enabling the other party to decrypt (unscramble) the information to read the contents of the message. A cryptographic algorithm, called a cipher, scrambles the information. A key is used with the cipher in order for someone to be able to encrypt and decrypt the message. The complexity of the cipher is not the root of the strength of security. Instead, the strength of security depends

---

3. CERT Coordination Center Web site (www.cert.org), Software Engineering Institute, Carnegie Mellon University, April 5, 2002.

on the length of the key. The longer the key, the more calculations must be performed in order to "break" it. Lightweight SSL transactions are typically performed with a 40-bit key. A 128-bit key provides stronger authentication. In fact, a 128-bit encryption is roughly 309,485,009,821,345,068,724,781,056 times stronger than 40-bit encryption because of the longer key length.[4] You can think of the key as a shared secret between the sender and the receiver. SSL has been used for electronic commerce interactions between Web browsers and Web servers. SSL is also commonly used to protect passwords for access to Web services.

Firewalls

For interactive services, the move from novelty to necessity means that personal, corporate, and institutional network administrators must be diligent about ensuring that only desired data traffic is flowing across the boundaries between the public network and their private networks. Firewall is a general term used to describe a set of technologies that manages inbound and outbound network traffic. Network security administrators can configure firewalls to block all, some, or no data traffic based on particular criteria established by their own security policies. There are many different and emerging forms of firewalls being established to meet the continuously changing threats to networks. Two general firewall techniques are covered here: packet filtering firewalls and application proxy firewalls.

Packet filtering firewalls look at all incoming and outgoing traffic for a network and only allow the data packets through the firewall's router that meet criteria established by the network administrator. Packet filtering firewalls are typically embedded in routers. Routers are the system elements that sit between the public network and the private networks "routing" the data traffic between the networks. Data traffic on IP-based networks break down into packets. A router

---

4. Netscape customer support knowledge base (http://help.netscape.com), America Online, August, 2002.

looks at each packet and determines where that packet should move next in the network. The firewall software at the router applies rules against the information in the packets to determine what should pass and what should be blocked. While firewalls do not constitute a foolproof method of security, the rule-based systems make for a solid first line of defense.

Application proxies provide another level of firewall security. Application proxies will only allow certain protocols to pass between the public and private networks. Protocols are the communication formats used by applications to transfer data. For example, there is the protocol used by Web servers (HTTP), the protocol used for general file transfer (FTP), and the protocol used by email (SMTP). Many consider application proxies a stronger form of security than packet filtering routers because application proxies block a certain class of activity from happening. For example, if you only want Web pages to travel out of your network, you could allow HTTP traffic out of your network, but block other activities such as general file transferring or email.

Firewalls as well as security technology continue to evolve over time. As more valuable assets are stored on networks, we should expect more individuals to try to illegally gain access to these assets. Evolving from novelty to necessity means that interactive services must take critical infrastructure technologies such as security to higher levels.

Other Security Technologies

The security technologies we have examined are just two technologies in an increasingly complex space. All aspects of integrated services will need stronger and stronger security as integrated services migrate from novelty to necessity. The data centers that the applications servers run in, the databases that store information, and communication networks through which information travels will continue to become more secure through enhancements in processes and technology.

Security can come at a price of performance and ease of use. It will be critical for the designers of security technologies to continue to raise the bar for those who would like to breach integrated services while not making it more prohibitive for people to derive value from their interactive services. This can be a challenging balancing act.

LEARNED BEHAVIORS

When people become truly dependent on services, people begin to change their behavior. This shift occurs especially when consumers begin to take such services for granted. Examples include water, sewer, electricity, and phone service for your home. Manufacturers can assume the presence of such services in the home and develop new devices based on the assumption that, for example, electricity is readily available. For integrated services, the shift in how consumers use devices puts a challenge before the designers and providers of devices and services. These new learned behaviors emerge from integrating interactive services so intimately into one's life that a new level of expectations are levied at the service provider. For example, the number of online banking customers grew from 1.2 million in 1998 to 14.9 million in 2001.[5] Increasing use of such online services will naturally lead to increased expectations, including ubiquitous access, privacy, reliance, and continuous service enhancement.

Ubiquitous Access

The implications of consumers gaining access to integrated services anywhere goes well beyond the challenges of simple access. Gaining access from anywhere can imply that a person wants to access the services not only from any place but also from multiple devices.

---

5. Yonish, Steve, with Jennifer Gordon. "Highlight, Consumer Tech Adoption Forecast," Boston: Forrester Research.

Having a common and consistent experience from these multiple devices creates significant challenges. For example, some mobile professionals want to be able to reach their email services from the personal computer, their mobile PDA, as well as their mobile phone. The challenges surrounding what functionality and capabilities are available on these different devices given their different user interfaces and mode of use are significant. One device may be full featured, while another may only allow you to read and send simple mail but exclude your ability to make attachments. To compound the challenge, ubiquitous access to integrated services creates issues surrounding the notion of privacy and personal information.

Access Points

Consumers have rising expectations that they can gain utility from their integrated services from anywhere they desire. This has resulted in an explosion in mobile devices and wireless networks as access points for the services.

Mobility

The need for mobility in devices challenges industrial design and human interface design with the limited real estate for such devices. Handheld gaming consoles, notebook computers, personal digital assistants, portable music players, and data-capable mobile phones all share the requirements for durability, duration, and interoperability.

Things that travel with owners get dropped and banged in ways that desktop phones and personal computers do not. This means that industrial design for these devices must be highly durable to take the punishment that comes from the demands of mobility. At the same time, no one wants to carry excess weight with them. The industrial design of the device must be as lightweight and compact as possible, as well as meet the current aesthetic demands. This demand pushes device manufacturers to find the right balance between lighter and stronger materials and device capabilities.

Another aspect of mobility is the ability to use the device for long periods of time without needing to connect to anything, even for power. This means that devices need to draw as little power as possible while providing the required experience. While we have seen dramatic improvements in processor speeds and memory, battery technology has not advanced at the same rate.

Finally, occasionally the consumer would like to be able to transfer information from their device to another person's device without needing to hook up cables. Technologies like infrared ports and local wireless networks via WiFi or Bluetooth address this need of communication across devices.

Consistency of Experience

Consumers may use multiple devices in a variety of places during the course of a day. A person wishes to gain access to interactive services at a time and place that is convenient for the consumer without considering the status of the network. Consumers use the network for a variety of tasks, ranging from looking up the status of a delivery to checking their email. Whether from a laptop computer, a mobile phone, or a wireless personal digital assistant, consumers demand the ability to reach such service whenever and wherever they may find themselves. One of the challenges for the service providers is designing a constant and easy-to-use human interface to access services independent of the device. The key elements of accessing interactive services—authentication and authorization—become a significant challenge.

Authentication

The service needs to know that the consumer is who the consumer claims to be before allowing access to an interactive service such as a Web service. There are many methods of authentication, but not all provide the same level of security or are easy to use from particular devices. For example, many Web services offer access via a desktop computer with the consumer using a user name and a password for identification. This method of authentication has obvious frailties. Any person with that consumer's password can gain access to the consumer's services and, potentially, personal information. It may also be difficult to use a username and password from devices such as a mobile phone where there is a keypad, but not a keyboard to enter the information.

One class of authentication under development is *biometric authentication*. Biometric authentication depends on a unique physical characteristic to identify someone. For example, this type of authentication can use voice, fingerprint, retinal imaging, or facial features to verify a person's identity. While more convenient for the end user than password authentication, biometric authentication still has significant interoperability issues with the standard ways authentication systems are managed today. It is anticipated that these challenges will be overcome in time. The advantages of biometric authentication for the end user are that the end user does not have to remember a password or carry a physical object, such as a passkey, with him or her. These forms of authentication can be easily forgotten or misplaced. Today, password-based authentication remains the most common identification technique used by interactive services.

Authorization

After identifying the user, the interactive service must match the identity of the user against what the person is authorized to do. Permissions surrounding authorization can be very complex and depend on characteristics of the individual. For example, services often check if the account in good standing and to what services have the subscriber purchased and are entitled. The service can also see if there are there limitations or parental controls that have been placed on the account. Authorization requires a tight coupling between the definition of the subscription or product, the subscriber's account, and the subscriptions in the account.

America Online (AOL) demonstrates how an interactive service uses authentication and authorization across multiple devices. AOL subscribers have access to a wide array of interactive services ranging from email to calendaring and instant messaging to stock portfolio management. Subscribers to AOL do not always find themselves in a situation where they can access these services through the traditional AOL client application that runs on personal computers. For example, an AOL subscriber may find himself or herself with a Web browser at a computer that doesn't have the AOL client application or sitting in front of their television at home.

AOL Anywhere provides different interfaces to an array of AOL services from multiple devices. For example, an AOL subscriber can use instant messaging from a mobile phone and also gain access to email from any Web browser. The subscriber uses their AOL screen name and password to gain access to the services, regardless of device. AOL then determines what functionality the consumer needs based on the account and what the device interface will allow.

Privacy

With the ability to authenticate and authorize subscribers from multiple access points comes greater exposure of personal information in the network. The proper use of personal information grows increasingly important. Interactive services must pay stringent attention to how the service handles subscribers' personal information or risk losing customers.

As we noted earlier, there is a natural desire for the providers of services to know as much as possible about their customer in order to provide the most relevant service. How that personal information is used and with whom it is shared are subject to privacy policies. Most privacy policies start from the concept of expressed disclosure. The subscriber must explicitly accept the terms of a provider's privacy policy. Most privacy policies invoke the concepts of asking for permission before ever sharing the information with others.

Watchdog entities such as TrustE have come into existence to provide independent privacy auditing to digital services. Companies agree to adhere to TrustE guidelines in order to use the TrustE brand to display their industry compliance with privacy rules. As in Europe, most likely the government will contribute to establishing standards, practices, and enforcement of privacy rules. The reality is that most privacy watchdog efforts today have not been strongly enforced. Until the enforcement surrounding privacy auditing is made stronger, the transition from novelty to necessity for many interactive services could be a slow one.

Reliance

As consumers continue to make integrated services a deeper part of their lives, they become more reliant on the availability and performance of the interactive services. The expectations of consumers are clear in a service relationship. To use the interactive service, consumers require service reliability, performance, continuity, and security.

Service Reliability

Service reliability breaks down into multiple components. Service availability is a key element to maintaining customer loyalty. A consumer must be able to access services whenever the consumer wishes. Since it is difficult to impossible to predict when a consumer is going to want to access the network, the service operator needs to assume availability twenty-four hours a day, seven days a week.

Another word for service availability is "uptime." Consumers expect an idealized uptime of 100 percent. The reality of ensuring that level of uptime is extremely resource intensive, requiring highly redundant systems. The reality is equipment will fail, humans will make mistakes, and systems require maintenance and upgrades. One hundred percent uptime over long periods of time is not economically achievable. The balancing act between the consumer and the service provider then becomes a question of what uptime is good enough. System administrators must balance how many "nines of uptime" is required to meet customer expectations.

PERCENTAGE OF MONTHLY UPTIME	ACTUAL TOTAL DOWNTIME
100	0 minutes
99.999	26 seconds
99.99	4 minutes, 19 seconds
99.9	43 minutes, 12 seconds
99	7 hours, 12 minutes

In a month with 30 days, there are 43,200 minutes. If a service is available for 99.999 percent of the time, or "five nines" of availability, then the service will not be available for a total of 26 seconds during the month. In comparison, if a service is available 99 percent of the time, the service would not be available for a total of 7 hours, 12 minutes during the same time period. To the consumer, 99.999 percent uptime (truly exceptional availability) is worthless if the rare failure happens during a critical time. Imagine needing to make an emergency 911 call. If that moment happens to fall within the 4 minutes and 19 seconds of downtime that month, the service has not met your needs. The importance of reliability pushes system administrators toward reaching as close as possible to 100 percent uptime.

Performance

To consumers, performance means how quickly a device or service responds to a request for action. For those who design and test devices and systems, there are many aspects to performance to take into account. Designers need to think first and foremost about the consumer experience and the consumer's expectations.

Perceived Performance versus Actual Performance

One dimension of performance to take into consideration is perceived performance versus actual performance. Actual performance means measuring the time taken for a desired response under established conditions. Perceived performance translates to a person's self-assessment of the amount of time taken for a system to respond under the same conditions. It's important to note that consumers have expectations around *perceived* performance, not actual performance. For example, if a person is provided some form of feedback while waiting for a response, then the consumer thinks the response is much faster simply because there is an indicator that activity is happening. If the consumer receives no feedback while waiting for a response, the consumer has much more time to contemplate the length of time waiting. Showing visual or audio progress toward completing a task leaves the consumer with the perception of greater performance.

Peak Load versus Average Load

Another dimension of performance is system behavior for peak load versus average load. Load means the amount of activity that is anticipated for a system. The number of simultaneous calls on the network represents the load on a phone system. For the Internet, network administrators measure load in the number of packets traveling across the network. It is important to remember that the true test of performance for interactive services comes under peak load conditions. At peak load, demand is at its greatest. Fail to meet performance expectations under peak load and consumers' confidence about becoming dependent on that service goes down dramatically. This is especially true for financial services, retail services, communication services, and live media distribution.

People base their performance expectations on their experience at the time of greatest need. As a result, the bar for consumers' performance expectations gets set by perceived performance under peak load conditions (see Figure 6-3).

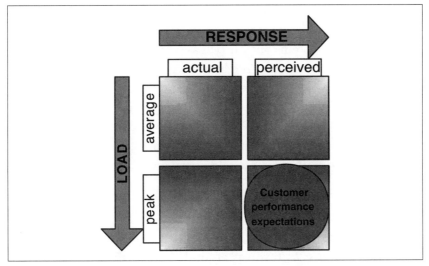

FIGURE 6-3. Customer Performance Expectation Matrix

Continuity

What happens when disaster strikes? If my device breaks, will I loose the information I had on it? How can I get all my information back? These are all the questions that surround disaster recovery, or in the business world "business continuity." More important information is making its way into interactive services, like transaction histories, health records, and legal documents. Consumers expect that this information is backed up and can be recovered in the event of a disaster. Disaster takes many forms. There are natural disasters, equipment failures, and human-made disasters.

Some aspects of continuity can seem trivial. For example, I store my favorite songs in an online music service. That music service might have a catastrophic failure, resulting in the servers hosting my songs being destroyed. I would expect that the music service will be able to recover my favorite songs when the service is reestablished. I would be less inclined to stay with the service if my information was lost as part of the service failure. Lost data become even more important with interactive services that involve the legal, financial, or health industries.

Maintaining system continuity is a complex blend of software and hardware recovery systems. At a basic level, the service administrator must focus on how quickly the service can be restored and the level of integrity that can be provided surrounding the data assets stored on behalf of the consumer. As users become more dependent on digital devices and services, consumers need assurances that a system failure can be corrected within a reasonable period of time.

Security

As interactive services evolve from novelty to necessity, one of people's greatest concerns revolves around the guardianship of private information. Service providers must secure personal information of subscribers as well as protect against malicious attacks on the systems. Companies can put in place privacy policies to define the parameters of reusing customer information. However, if the information itself is not safe within the systems, the service provider fails to meet the consumer expectation for the protection of personal information.

Protecting Information and Systems

Identity theft is a growing concern throughout the world. Identity theft occurs when an unauthorized person assumes the identity of another individual. Once an identity is successfully broached, the person can gain access to financial assets. For example, a person who gains access to a victim's financial services can run up significant debt in the victim's name. Such behavior can lead to damaged credit ratings for the victim and years of difficulties dealing with other financial institutions. Consumers place more of their life's information in interactive services. There is a corresponding need for services to prevent identity theft for their customers. Preventing identity theft requires stronger authentication technologies, as well as checks and balances within the business logic of systems.

The final element of security for a service lies in protecting the system from destructive programmatic attacks such as viruses and worms. These pieces of programming code are created with the intent to cause harm to other systems. For example, a virus can consume computing resources or erase information that is already stored. While it is impossible to prevent all programmatic attacks, services must devote a significant effort to blocking viruses from service systems.

INTERACTIVE SERVICES AND CONSUMER EXPECTATIONS

It is simple reality that the first few generations of interactive services will fall short of consumer expectations. Consumers push devices and networks to the limits of their capabilities. Initially, networks will fail and services will sometimes lose customers who are annoyed by dips in performance or security. However, the lessons learned in maintaining service-level systems that handle multiple access points drives interactive services toward fast and continuous improvement. The greatest motivation for the service provider is and always will be the customer. The more the customer depends on the device and uses the service, the higher the standards for the service provider. These high standards form the foundation for creating interactive experiences that customers integrate into their daily lives.

Targeting the Interactive Consumer

Consumers incorporate integrated services into daily routines when the benefits provided reflect their real needs. Focusing exclusively on enabling technologies rather than the customer needs is a common mistake made by designers of new devices and applications. While technology enables companies to provide new classes of integrated services, attention to classic product marketing processes leads to the integrated service's success in the marketplace. The ongoing cycle of consumers adopting new devices, developing new behaviors, and forming new expectations results in a constantly changing market. New customers with shifting expectations provide significant challenges to both the designers and marketers of integrated services. Focusing on customer needs rather than the cool new technology while designing and packaging integrated services helps ensure success for an integrated service.

After reading this chapter, you should have a good understanding of the following topics:

- The role of product marketing for integrated services

- The roles that context, cost, and clear communication play in the success of integrated services

- The characteristics of change in integrated services

BACK TO BASICS

It can sometimes be hard to believe that simple rules compose the heart of an integrated service's complex array of technologies, business models, and consumer behavior. Peter Drucker wrote that the two primary functions of a company are marketing and innovation.[1] Everything else is simply a cost to the business. While the most visible aspect of marketing is product advertising, product marketing is arguably the most important marketing function carried out for an integrated service.

Effective product marketing for integrated services consists of the following elements:

■ **Product**—the definition of the integrated service in terms of features, benefits, packaging, and its positioning to the market.

■ **Price**—the cost to the customer that can include various pricing structures and financing options.

■ **Place**—the channels through which the customer can obtain the integrated service, such as a retail store, mail order catalog, or from a Web site.

■ **Promotion**—the means by which customers learn about the presence of the integrated service and incentives for buying the integrated service. Advertising, contests, and press releases all fall into this category of marketing.

Technology acts as an enabler and supporter for the goals of the product marketer. For example, advances in technology make it possible to provide greater functionality or higher quality at a lower price. At the end of the day, the customer is buying the benefits they perceive in the integrated service, not the technology in and of itself.

---

1. Drucker, Peter. "The Essential Drucker." New York: HarperBusiness, 2001, page 20.

Product

Integrated services have unique characteristics that impact marketing decisions concerning product, price, place, and promotion. First, integrated services impact decisions made around product definition. Integrated services are typically a blend of hardware (such as devices) and services (such as network access and content). This means that most integrated services are technically complex by definition. Consider the components of a telematics integrated service. As noted in Chapter 5, telematics gives automotive manufacturers the ability to provide digital services to the car owner as an option on the automobile. Two examples are OnStar's automatic collision notification and Wingcast's planned gas-station locator. Both these integrated services combine embedded systems within the automobile, data networks, and a service provider system. An integrated service that ties together device, network, and applications requires a certain level of compatibility between each element. While this integration is highly complex, the customer does not value the complexity in and of itself. Typically, the consumer wants to receive the value from using the integrated service, but does not desire to appreciate the amount of complexity that has been integrated in order to provide it. The customer wants to simply have OnStar deliver the appropriate information after a collision and does not need to know how the notification occurs. The challenge in product definition for integrated services lies in blending components that provide compelling benefits while maintaining intuitive to the consumer. Lack of success in getting the product definition correct leads to increased customer support requests, decreased use, and leaves opportunity for competitors in the marketplace.

Price

The second area of focus is price. The cost structures of developing, testing, and deploying products, such as a consumer electronics device, and a communications network, such as a wireless telecommunications network, are very different. Yet, when a consumer wants to buy a "cell phone," most of the time they are talking about the device, the network, and the services that run on top of both. A complex value chain exists within an integrated service between the providers of devices, networks, and service and their respective vendors. Everyone needs to get paid, but paid in a way that scales with the cost of the component to the overall integrated service. A difficult balance comes into play between the following elements:

- How consumers value such integrated services

- How consumers are willing to pay for such integrated services

- How the providers of such integrated services and their respective vendors can profit.

Complicating the pricing decision is the sheer cost of integrating many of these early integrated services. According to Jupitermedia Research's cost model, the total annualized cost per telematics subscriber is approximately $310 for embedded systems and $250 for integrated systems over an average of 3.5 years of ownership. The upfront costs—including equipment and setup—account for between 85 and 90 percent of this total. Ongoing service costs add another annual $35 per subscriber, the majority of which falls under customer service calls. For example, in 2002, OnStar experienced 14,250 calls per month and 375 calls per month, respectively, for roadside dispatches and stolen-vehicle recover calls. Navigation routing calls clocked in at 200,000 calls monthly.[2] Acceptable pricing for the consumer becomes difficult when balancing between the costs of the

---

2. Ask, Julie, with Jay Horwitz, Elif Akcayli, Corina Matiesanu, Michael Gartenberg. "In-Vehicle Applications: Telematics Enables Contextual Services and Operational Efficiencies Visio Report," New York: Jupitermedia Research, April 19, 2002.

different components. Consumer costs can include the following:

◧ Ongoing fees for the use of network resources. These charges may come in the form of being billed for minutes or packets on telecommunication networks or in the form of monthly flat fees for Internet service.

◧ Pay-per-use or subscriptions fees for value-added applications or services above what is provided in a base package.

◧ The cost of the device. This typically consists of either the consumer paying for the full price of the device or having some or all of the device costs subsidized by one of the parties that is making ongoing network, application, or service revenues from the consumer.

With many components that have different cost structures (devices, networks, applications/services), it can be challenging to put forward pricing models that are easily understood (and accepted) by consumers. The key lies in understanding the customer value for the integrated service. For example, AT&T is working with DaimerChrysler AG (Chrysler), the world's third largest automobile manufacturer, to provide a telematics integrated service to address the consumer need of hands-free in-vehicle communication. The integrated service is an onboard system that interconnects the vehicle bus for audio integration, local storage for contact information, and Bluetooth connectivity for wireless access to AT&T's cellular network. Chrysler plans to price the system by charging for the equipment in the low range for integrated platforms (low range being between $300 and $1,100). Picking the appropriate price in that range requires pricing the value that the consumer places on the following:

◧ Safety while talking on cell phones while driving

◧ Ease of communication while driving

◧ Access to voice services while driving

The target audience for device or delivery mechanism also affects pricing for an integrated service. ATX Technologies provides a routing assistance integrated service that BMW distributes under the private label BMW Assist as part of its luxury automobile options. BMW Assist features include consumer routing assistance, automatic collision notification, and remote diagnostics. BMW attracts buyers to the option using a two-tier annual subscription model: the basic security package for $225 (consumer routing assistance, automatic collision notification, and remote diagnostics) and the information service package for $350 (includes email and Web access). Targeting flexible package pricing toward a demographic already in the market for a luxury product has resulted in early success. In 2002, the company reported a 70 percent renewal rate for subscriptions.[3]

Place and Promotion

The type of integrated service also affects place and promotion. In order for an integrated service to be successful, consumers need to be able to purchase the integrated service through convenient channels. Promotional campaigns can educate the market about the merits of the integrated service as well as stimulate demand. The consumer acquires integrated services through a physical retail store, a customer-initiated request by phone or Internet, or via a bundled into a larger purchase platform. In the previous telematics examples, Chrysler distributes the hands-free communication integrated service and BMW ships the ATX product under the BMW Assist brand. Consumer electronics retailers distribute many integrated services, such as game consoles, digital cameras, mobile phones, PDAs, and personal video recorders. Integrated services that are viewed primarily as a utility

---

3. Ask, Julie, with Jay Horwitz, Elif Akcayli, Corina Matiesanu, Michael Gartenberg. "In-Vehicle Applications: Telematics Enables Contextual Services and Operational Efficiencies Visio Report," New York: Jupitermedia Research, April 19, 2002.

service (such as home security systems) have their devices delivered as part of an installation and activation process.

Promotion primarily serves the purpose of educating the marketplace about the merits of the integrated service as well as helping to stimulate demand. Promotion takes many creative forms. For example, promotions surrounding the cost of the device can reduce the cost of entry for the consumer and drive adoption. Integrated services like digital television services, game consoles, and mobile phones promote services heavily since most of their revenue comes from service relationships with the consumer. Another common promotion is a free trial period for the service component of the integrated service. For example, AOL frequently runs promotions to allow new subscribers a limited time of free access to the service before billing. Promotions target customer retention as well as customer acquisition. Since much of the revenue generated for integrated services come from on-going fees, the lifetime value of the customer is extremely important. Promotions around customer retention often involve discounts or rewards to existing bills and bundling new features for a customer. As described in earlier chapters, many cable operators consider VOD a key element in retaining customers for the cable service. According to a Forrester Research report, cable operators report that customer churn (the percentage of subscribers dropping digital cable service in a given month) drops approximately 2 percent in VOD systems. A cable operator could offer VOD as a new feature or at a discount to prevent customer attrition. Likewise, satellite operators see personal video recorders (PVRs) as a similar promotional tool for customer retention. One satellite operator reported that "Our PVR subscribers never leave us."[4] Promotions serve as a powerful tool for both attracting new customers and retaining existing subscribers.

Meeting the needs of all the parties in an integrated service while delivering a strong consumer value proposition presents a significant

4. Bernoff, Josh. "How Cable TV Can Beat Satellite," Boston: Forrester Research, Inc., April 2002.

challenge. Competitive integrated services will continue to become increasingly relevant to a person's daily life, moving from novelty to necessity. As such, addressing issues surrounding context, cost, and communication will be key to defining the most effective mix of product, price, place, and promotion in the future.

CONTEXT

Any integrated service must be relevant to the customer in order for the customer to derive sufficient value to purchase the integrated service. Integrated services provide greater relevance and value to consumers through sensitivity to context. Context takes into account the person and his or her environment in order to best meet the needs of the consumer. For example, the core consumer value for telematic integrated services lies in the context of its use. Hands-free communication while driving has a higher value proposition than hands-free communication while standing in line at the grocery store. Given the context of driving, the consumer values the integrated services because of the benefits of safety, comfort, and ease of use.

Environmental context elements, such as the physical, temporal, and cultural environment must be taken into account if an integrated service is to be successfully deployed. Beyond environmental context, there is personal context that can dramatically enhance the value the consumer will derive from the integrated service.

Designing an integrated service that takes into account the environment in which it is intended to be used is a critical success factor. For example, telematics integrated services must consider the distance between the driver and the communication device, as well as ambient noise from radios and the road itself. Without taking into consideration the environmental context for usage, the integrated service risks losing relevance with the consumer market. For example, Apple Computer had all the necessary components for the PDAs in the early 1990s. The first Apple Newton was too large and heavy and emphasized a user interface (handwriting recognition) that did not meet consumer's expectations (extremely high accuracy). It did not address the environment in which the consumer would use the device—such as on the road in a hurry. The PDA did not achieve commercial sales expectations until Palm provided a device that met users' needs. Palm provided a device that was light, could fit in your pocket or purse, and provided shorthand for making entries into the device.

Another aspect of physical context to consider is the number of individuals using the device. Whether a group or an individual uses the device dramatically impacts how the device intends to display content or information. For example, if the content of information needs to be presented to a group, having the equivalent of a postage stamp of screen real estate is not going to meet the consumer's needs. A larger display is required. Other aspects of group versus individual use include privacy, user specific privileges, and personalization.

The final aspect of physical context to consider revolves around the harshness of the environment in which the integrated service is expected to perform. For example, a global positioning integrated service to be used in remote areas of Alaska or Siberia will have different industrial design demands than a PVR that gets placed on a shelf in your entertainment system cabinet. The mobile GPS device will need to be highly mobile, highly durable, and able to gain access to the GPS satellite network from very remote locations. The use of a PVR can assume the presence of a power source and that it will not be moved often, but that it may be "always on."

Devices, networks, applications, and services must also enable consumers to use the integrated service seamlessly within the consumer's cultural environment. Cultural contexts become even more important when taking international considerations into account. The way text is displayed, the way a device sounds, or even the logos that exist on the device's user interface must all be taken into consideration for any country in which the integrated service is intended to be used.

Pricing

The sellers of integrated services will always try to price their integrated services to "what the market will bear." However, integrated services are often additive to a consumer's existing cost of living. Integrated services do not substitute food, clothing, and shelter . . . or even entertainment costs like cable subscriptions. In addition, the true cost of an integrated service can be complicated between start-up costs, ongoing costs, and opportunity costs. Product marketers that are sensitive to consumer costs are much more likely to be successful in the consumer market place.

Start-up Costs

From a consumer's perspective, this is the most visible and up-front cost of the three cost components. Start-up costs are the initial time and money that is required of the customer to purchase the integrated service. In one researcher's cost model, of the $310 annualized cost per telematics subscriber, between 85 and 90 percent goes to start-up costs.[5] Start-up costs can be money spent on purchasing a device at retail, an activation fee, or purchasing the first software or service to be used with the device. Start-up costs are often subsidized for consumers, since the true cost of the components in an integrated service can be high enough to prevent consumer adoption. For example, many providers of digital television will underwrite the cost of the digital television set-top box in order to reduce the initial costs for the subscriber.

Ongoing Costs

There can be service, maintenance, or ongoing costs associated with the integrated service, either in addition to or exclusive of start-up

---

5. Ask, Julie, with Jay Horwitz, Elif Akcayli, Corina Matiesanu, Michael Gartenberg. "In-Vehicle Applications: Telematics Enables Contextual Services and Operational Efficiencies Visio Report," New York: Jupitermedia Research, April 19, 2002.

costs. Some of these charges may come in the form of monthly sub-scription fees. Other costs can be buying additional modules to run with the integrated service. For example, game consoles are typically priced aggressively at or below cost in order to reduce the barrier to entry for the consumer and meet competitive price points in the market place. The ongoing cost to the consumer can be significant since they will be purchasing new games to play with the console. Many online services have subscription or recurring base fees asso-ciated with their integrated services. While the cost of admission might be low, the ongoing costs could be significant.

Someone who buys a device for less than $100, but with a $10-per-month subscription, will pay more for the subscription ($120) than they did for the device itself. Consumers are sensitive to on-going costs and often balk at the commitment of the billing rela-tionship. (See Figure 7-1 for the difference between perceived and actual cost of ownership.) It is best to have a scalable pricing struc-ture for ongoing costs based on the value that the consumer is de-riving from the integrated service and the incremental cost of pro-viding the service. Later in this chapter, we discuss NTT DoCoMo's iMode integrated service that has effectively priced ongoing charges for their integrated service in a way that optimizes their returns and margin.

Opportunity Costs

Opportunity costs are often the most elusive and difficult costs for the consumer to quantify. One way of looking at opportunity cost is asking the question "what alternative are you passing up in or-der to spend time and resources on this integrated service?" Many integrated services are designed for enhanced productivity or enter-tainment. If a customer does not find the integrated service effective, the customer will look for other alternatives. For example, if it takes a consumer too long to learn a complex interactive television inter-face, the consumer may discard the new technology as too difficult to use in relation for the features gained. The designers of integrated

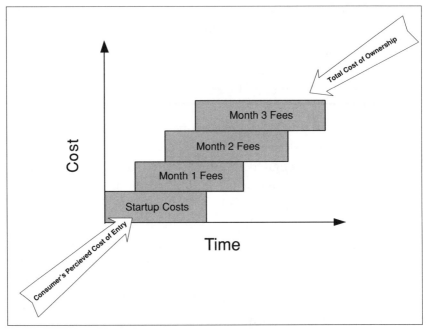

FIGURE 7-1. Perceived versus Actual Cost of Ownership

services must be sensitive and respectful of consumers' opportunity costs.

COMMUNICATION

The communication between the interactive consumer and the providers of the integrated service provides the information required to price, support, and enhance successful product. The first tier of communications, advertising and promotions, makes the customer aware of the integrated service through education about benefits and providing incentives for purchase. The second tier of customer communications lies in customer care and support. The final area of communication involves cross-sell and up-sell tactics to lure the customer into more services.

Advertising and Promotional Communications

Typically, the first interaction between a consumer and the provider of an integrated service is through advertising or promotional marketing communications. These communications enable the provider of the integrated service to tell perspective customers about the relevancy of the integrated service to the consumer. The challenge for the provider of integrated services lies in the technical complexity of the integrated service. It can be difficult to explain the value of the integrated service without complicating the message with technical background. For example, when marketing mobile networks in the United States, wireless carriers initially positioned the mobile data services as the "mobile Internet." This type of positioning focuses on the communications network and not the benefits to the consumer. The Internet experience in North America is primarily experienced through a personal computer with a large screen and a full keyboard. The data services experience on a mobile phone is very different from the PC Internet experience—the data input mechanism and screen display vary greatly between the PC and the cell phone. As a result, the expectations of the consumer get set unrealistically and ultimately lead to disappointment. In many Asian countries, such as Japan and South Korea, the mobile data services are marketed via their applications and content. This tactic conveys the actual benefit to the end user and does not concentrate on the technical means by which they gain access to the benefit.

Customer Care and Support

Many companies view customer care and support interactions as a burden and cost of doing business. More progressive companies view customer care and support interactions as an opportunity to retain a customer and to derive a greater lifetime value associated with the customer. Many companies are deploying systems that enable customers to be able to receive customer care and support through automated self-service applications. When such methods are used, the customer can often be trained in the effective use of the integrated service (if user error was the root of the problem), or they can learn at a pace that is conducive to the customer's schedule or circumstances.

Effective customer care and support can also be used as a feedback loop for learning about how to improve the integrated service as well as learning about how customers are using the integrated service. It is often the case with integrated services that they can be used in unintended ways. These new ways of using the integrated service are new learned behaviors that the provider of the integrated service needs to know about if they are to understand the next shifts in customer expectations.

A significant challenge in an integrated service lies in effective customer support for a multiple component system. In an integrated service that combines a device, network support, and applications, customer service issues can be difficult to track down and address. It's critical for each component to provide clear lines of communication between companies to solve a customer problem that might span multiple products. The consumer doesn't care where the error lies in an integrated service. Getting bumped between different customer care service centers without a clear resolution leaves customers with a poor impression of the integrated service.

NTT DoCoMo's iMode[6]

One of the most compelling success stories for an integrated service is NTT DoCoMo's iMode service. NTT DoCoMo is Japan's largest wireless carrier, providing wireless communication services to over 48 million subscribers. iMode is the mobile data services integrated service from DoCoMo. This service proved sensitive to consumer issues of context, cost, and value communications and resulted in a wild success. iMode went from zero subscribers in 1999 to 32 million

---

6. DoCoMo corporate Web site (www.DoCoMo.com), July 16, 2002.

subscribers in 2002. What did iMode do to experience such rapid consumer adoption?

First, DoCoMo started with the devices. The new mobile data services required that DoCoMo customers adopt new phones since the traditional cell phones were not capable of supporting the new data service. DoCoMo decided that in order to get broad adoption, the service would target young women as the initial market. DoCoMo made the gamble that young women, as strong consumers in Japan, would lead the adoption wave for the device. It is important to understand that this was fairly novel at the time since most technology marketers traditionally target young men. DoCoMo selected an industrial design for the phone that they thought would be most attractive to young women. Taking into account the physical and cultural context of the target market, the resulting industrial design was a light, thin portable phone. This selection of target market also drove some of the early decisions around content and services. Rather than marketing the iMode service as "the mobile Internet" as in the United States, DoCoMo emphasized its communications, entertainment, and information services. DoCoMo used a pricing structure that let the consumer determine how much of the service the consumer wanted to obtain while providing incentive to third-party developers who would provide the new content and applications that consumers would ultimately come to value.

By clearly targeting their core markets, iMode was able to provide valuable context to decisions around the choice of phone design, content providers, and service integrated services. DoCoMo was able to price the service in such a way that a broad consumer base could afford to try the device first and then decide to pay more if the consumer derived more usage and value from the service. Finally, iMode was successful in communicating a clear value proposition to the marketplace for the use of the mobile data service. NTT DoCoMo's iMode demonstrates the results of being sensitive to context, cost, and communications.

THE EVOLUTION OF INTEGRATED SERVICES

Through the course of this book, we have explored the diverse and rich domain of integrated services. The continued evolution from analog devices and networks to digital devices and networks leads to more capable integrated services at lower price points. However, if the provider of the integrated service is not sensitive to context, cost, and communication about the integrated service, it is likely that the integrated service will not find successful adoption in the consumer marketplace. Successful integrated services take on characteristics that will increase the integrated service's personal relevance to the consumer.

People increasingly rely on integrated services for "mission critical" portions of their daily lives. Safety integrated services that range from home security systems and portable health monitoring to roadside assistance and automobile maintenance monitoring are just some of the examples of integrated services that can create serious consequences when things don't work as designed. Concepts such as systems continuity, security, reliability, and availability will increasingly become selling points.

The continued integration of digital pictures, video, and music into daily routines fuels the evolution of devices, networks, and services. Challenges surrounding copyright laws, digital rights management, and the storage for increasingly large amount of media-rich data will need to be tackled in the years ahead to ensure broad consumer adoption. While there are many benefits to integrated services, these benefits need to be weighed against the challenges that exist in deploying such integrated services. There will be increasing concerns about security, privacy, and the protection of intellectual property. The costs surrounding such integrated services will be barriers to the less economically fortunate. And finally, a new infrastructure with similarly reliable services as public utilities needs to be established to gain full customer confidence. These challenges can be overcome by understanding and responding to customer demand and through cooperation between components of an integrated service.

Integrated services continue to take advantage of the multiple rich media formats that the devices and networks can support. By blending the benefits of the device, the network, and the application, integrated services provide consumers with new tools to enhance the consumer's lifestyle.

 # Bibliography: Interactive Expectations

Ask, Julie, with Jay Horwitz, Elif Akcayli, Corina Matiesanu, Michael Gartenberg. "In-Vehicle Applications: Telematics Enables Contextual Services and Operational Efficiencies Visio Report," New York: Jupitermedia Research, April 19, 2002.

Behr, Mary E. "E3 2002 Preview: Video Games to Take Center Stage," PC Magazine, May 20, 2002.

Bernoff, Josh. "Cable's On-Demand Salvation," Boston: Forrester Research, Inc., April 2001.

Bernoff, Josh. "How Cable TV Can Beat Satellite, April 2002," Boston: Forrester Research, Inc., April 2002.

CERT Coordination Center Web site (www.cert.org), Software Engineering Institute, Carnegie Mellon University, April 5, 2002.

DoCoMo corporate Web site (www.DoCoMo.com), July 16, 2002.

Drucker, Peter. "The Essential Drucker," New York: HarperBusiness, 2001.

FCC Wireless 911 Requirements, Federal Communications Commission, January 2001.

Forrester Research, Inc., Consumer Survey, "Devices & Access, 2002 Online Survey," Boston: Forrester Research, Inc., 2002.

Forrester Research, Inc., Consumer Survey, "Forrester's Consumer Technographics 2002 North America Benchmark Study," Boston: Forrester Research, Inc., 2002.

General Motors OnStar corporate Web site, www.generalmotors.com, July 15, 2002.

Gluck, Marissa, and Nikki Lewis, Ari Mayerfield, Adrienne Piras, Claudine Singer, Joe Laszlo, Michael May, Seamus McAteer. "Interactive Advertising on Post-PC Platforms: Emphasizing Modal Marketing," New York: Jupitermedia Research.

Health Care Financing Administration, Office of the Actuary, March 2001.

ISO in Figures, International Organization of Standards, January 2002.

Jackson, Paul. "Consumer Devices & Services Europe April 2002 Data Overview: Covers PCs, Net Access, Mobiles, iDTV, And Brands," Boston: Forrester Research, Inc., April 2002.

Kolko, Jed. "Who Consumers Trust With Personal Data," Boston: Forrester Research, Inc., June 7, 2002.

Kelley, Christopher M. "Retail & Media April 2001 Data Overview: Covers Email Marketing, eCommerce Growth, And Print Media Cannibalization," Boston: Forrester Research, Inc., April 2002.

Netscape customer support knowledge base (http://help.netscape.com), America Online, 2002.

SETI@Home Web site (http://setiathome.ssl.berkeley.edu/), July 15, 2002.

Yonish, Steve. "Highlight, Consumer Tech Adoption Forecast," Boston: Forrester Research, Inc.

Yonish, Steve. "Benchmark May 2002 Data Overview: Covers Digital Decade Forecasts, Device Ownership, Security and Wireless," Boston: Forrester Research, Inc., May 2002.

Index